M000312920

West of
Goose
Island

A Chicago Story

Richard S. Post

© Richard S. Post, 2013

Copyright © Richard S. Post
All rights reserved.

ISBN: 0989560805
ISBN 13: 9780989560801

Library of Congress Control Number: 2013911634
Post & Post LLC
Paradise Valley, AZ

Table of Contents

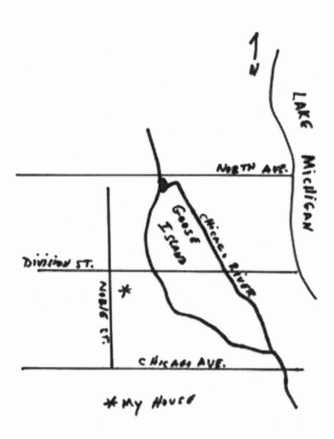

* MY HOUSE

Forward

I t was a good time to be a kid! The streets and alleys of Chicago provided lots of opportunities for adventure, and we learned about life on those streets. I grew up believing America was great and our block was even better. It shaped who I was and who I would become as an adult.

I lived in several different neighborhoods in what, at that time, was known to us as the "near north side." Division and Ashland, Palmer Square, and Humboldt Park figure prominently in these stories. These places were directly west of Goose Island. It was a Chicago landmark for the working poor.

Goose Island was a place with dirty factories, animal-rendering plants, gas storage tanks, and all sorts of businesses that polluted the air, our neighborhood, and the water in the Chicago River that flowed on all sides of the island. My grandmother's house on Throop Street faced factories and railroad tracks that were a buffer against the dirty, toxic work that was done there. Our house was the first stop after the island. The blocks around my house were the starting point for the immigrants who were beginning their lives in America.

While I was living on Throop Street, being so close to the island was never something you thought much about. Black dust was always on the windowsills, tables, and sheets that were drying on lines strung between buildings. Living next to it, the island was noticeable from the smells that would float over us when the wind came from the east.

Goose Island was always with us, as the boogeyman our parents would threaten us with if we didn't perform well in school or were mis-behaving. Once you smelled the raw animal odors from the rendering plants, you wanted nothing to do with even living near the island. "Keep it up and you'll be living on Goose Island," our parents would tell us.

Not a pleasant thought.

I only was on the island once, although going to the beach on the Division Street bus, I crossed it many times.

I was ten in the summer of 1950. Kasz, my good friend from our block, and I walked down the dirty street along the railroad tracks over to Division Street. We climbed down the bridge girders to the island. He wanted to swim. When we were on the island, we clambered down the pilings and onto a small patch of wet grass at the water's edge. There were small bubbles coming up from the dark water. He took off his jeans and T-shirt.

"I'm not going in there," I told him.

He went in anyway, diving into the black water. He came up almost immediately and swam back. I had to help pull him up out of the water.

"It feels funny in there, the water is too warm and soapy feeling," he said.

After his swim we ended up walking back to the Division Street YMCA so he could take a shower and clean the black scum off his back and neck. It never did come off his T-shirt, but you couldn't see it inside his jeans.

When the *Creature from the Black Lagoon* opened a few years later at a Loop theater, I thought about Kasz diving into the water on Goose Island. The river and the lagoon looked the same in black and white. The creature could have been lurking at Goose Island; no question.

Being surrounded by water that looked bad did not make the island an inviting place to go. It was, however, certainly something to be threatened with. It formed a natural barrier between all the riches the city had to offer in the Loop, the Gold Coast, the museums and the near north side, and the place where all the new immigrants lived west of Goose Island.

The three neighborhoods where these stories take place build upon a variety of experiences I found there.

Each of these places had a unique character, ethnic composition, and style during the 1940s and early 1950s. I tried to recreate the feel of that time and place as seen through the eyes of a young schoolboy before he started high school.

I have set down my recollections of the friends, relatives, and neighbors with as much accuracy as my memory and Chicago historical records permit. In some cases, composite characters have been used for privacy or legal considerations. The facts behind each situation are presented absolutely as real in fact as they are in my memory. I would hope that anyone reading these accounts and finds what they believe to be an error, contact me to set the record straight. Maybe my memory is not what it used to be!

Looking back on some of the things we did as kids growing up on the streets, I wonder why we are still alive. We took lots of chances, had broken bones, shattered dreams, and many wonderful friends. We learned about life; some of it was pretty raw and close to the bone, but we survived without bike helmets, training wheels, and uniforms for every sport we played in the street. New Keds and jeans were a luxury.

The street where my grandmother's house was located is now the Division Street Accident Investigation Site on the Kennedy Expressway. In fact, the entire block were we lived, built forts, played games, and dodged cars is now gone. The Polish people who lived there moved farther west in the city or out to the western suburbs. The same is true for Palmer Square and Humboldt Park that are now heavily Hispanic. Maybe fifty years from now someone will be writing about growing up in that Hispanic neighborhood for the next wave of immigrants who are starting their lives in Chicago.

Some people still talk about it taking a village to raise children properly. In the '40s and '50s, it was the nuns, the grocers, the buscias, the aunts, the uncles, and anyone who hung their heads out the windows watching what went on in the streets who made all the difference in neighborhood life in Chicago. They kept the streets safe, told your parents if you were doing something wrong, and made sure that no strangers came into where we lived without someone knowing about it. Our doors were seldom locked.

Don't get me wrong; everything was not all roses growing up. There was lots of disease: scarlet fever, polio, TB, rheumatic heart, lockjaw, rabies, typhoid, and pneumonia. I knew kids or parents that had them or died from them. We didn't have drug problems, but drunks were all over the place. Bums didn't come west past Ashland Avenue when we lived on Throop Street, but they were a part of our lives.

Some people would consider my Uncle Stanley to be a bum who just happened to have a mother that took care of him when he was drunk.

There was also crime. But, our version of neighborhood watch kept it to a minimum on our streets. Did kids get beaten by their parents for disobeying, talking back or for bad conduct? Sure, but they probably needed it. We all did once in a while, and most of us turned out OK.

We were poor people who didn't really know just how poor we were. We lived the way everyone else did. Everyone worked hard, parents made sure that their kids went to school, learned English, and followed the "Be American, Speak English" rule in their homes. While the fathers would sit around on the stoops in summer and drink beer, they went to work every day, sick or not, to try "getting ahead." People would sit on their front stoops on Throop and Cortez Streets but not on Albany or around Palmer Square. The neighborhoods there were different and filled with lots of different ethnic groups. People didn't seem to visit quite as much or even say "hello" to each other on the street.

What does a ten-year-old kid know about ethnic differences? What people think about or economics?

I knew when I felt safe, when people were fair, and when someone was being a real friend. There were kids who wanted everything for themselves and didn't like to share or would give you broken things to play with while they used the good stuff. Mothers who didn't want you to play in their house or with their kids. You knew which stores were nice to kids and would lend you a few pennies to get a comic book or Lindy when you were short. You remembered them and spent your money with them when you had it. If a puppy can tell if someone is treating them OK, why wouldn't kids be able to do at least as well?

Be American, Speak English

My grandmother lived on the second floor in the front building on the two-house lot that faced N. Throop Street. She lived there in a small three-room flat with Josie, another even older blind woman that never went out of the house. Summer would be boiling hot, but Josie would stay in her darkened room and listen to the radio blaring Polish church programs. In winter she would be bundled up in layers of sweaters doing the same thing day in, day out, all the time. There were always votive candles burning that made the apartment smell like church. I was glad we lived across the gangway in the rear building and didn't see or hear her every day.

Listening to her loud radio from her open window, my cousins and I learned to sing and hum the Polish version of Ava Maria before we even knew that it was really not a Polish song. Josie, like my grandmother, never learned to speak more than a few words of English. Josie died in 1948 and my grandmother in 1956.

It was easy to live in Chicago and never learn another language other than the one you arrived there speaking. The city is a collection of neighborhoods that placed a high value on people from one nationality sticking together. Poles lived with Poles, Russians with Russian, Ukrainians with Ukrainians, and Irish with Irish. Growing up there, we didn't know that there was another way of living; we thought it was a great place to be. There were lots of kids to play with, the schools were easy to walk to, and not many bad things happened in your own neighborhood.

My grandmother was always working around her buildings to keep up her six rental apartments. She had help from my uncle Stanley when he was not too drunk to stand up. They yelled and cursed at each other all day long in both Polish and English. That really helped me learn lots of good words in both languages.

Most of the parents, including mine, worked all the time. "Make sure you get to school on time," would be the last thing I would hear in the morning or it would be, "Make sure you come home right after school."

My parents tried to make sure they knew what we were doing all the time, but unless the weather was really cold, there were always lots of babushkas standing around outside that would always tell your mom what you were doing. It was hard to get away with anything.

Parents expected us to be responsible but set limits on how far that freedom would go. It was OK to walk across several busy streets to get to school but not all right to go to a friend's house to play unless my parents gave permission for a home visit. Kids were not allowed to make that kind of decision. "Where were they from; what city; which village in the old country; were they 'good people?'" my parents would ask every time the question of a home visit was raised, so the issue did not come up very often. There was also the question of where in the neighborhood did they live, near us or on the borderline?

It was definitely what I would later learn was called "class consciousness" that families brought with them from the old country. My family was always sorting people according to whether they were *szlachta* or *nizsze klasy* and we were not allowed to play with either of them because they were either too high or too low class. Jews were not even to be mentioned in the house but since we didn't have any in the neighborhood it was never an issue for us kids. Most of the Jews near us were Russian. They lived around North Avenue and Ashland Avenue and owned lots of stores and shops.

Milwaukee Avenue cut through the neighborhood like an arrow. The EL was underground beneath the street and took people east to the loop and west to Logan Square. It was the major dividing line for our neighborhood on the southwest. The elevated section of the Burlington Northern Railroad tracks cut us off on the east, while Division Street formed the northern boundary. My grandmother's house faced the tracks and the factories where they loaded the furniture they produced onto trains that headed all over the country. The west end of our neighborhood was dominated by Noble Street, Holy Trinity Church, along with its grammar and high school, and three blocks of factories and shops that lined both sides of Milwaukee Avenue and Division Street where they converged at Ashland Avenue.

The neighborhood did not have a special Chicago name like, *Back of the Yards, Near North, Gold Coast, Evergreen Park,* or even *Rogers Park.* We were even cut off from Goose Island by the train tracks and the Chicago River. If someone ever asked where you lived, you told them, "Division and Ashland," and that said it all. The triangle corner where Division, Ashland, and Milwaukee Avenues all met really had its own identity as a destination. The El stop was there, a movie theater, Walgreens Drugs, Goldblatt's department store, shoe stores, a bank, the white-tiled Dziennik Chicagoski Polish Alliance newspaper building, a magic store, a White Castle, a large newspaper and magazine stand, and the best soda shop in the city. It was the central shopping area for the near north side of Chicago and the one closest to the loop. If you could not find what you wanted there, you got on the El and went downtown.

In many ways our small neighborhood was landlocked in what acted like a Polish village that was transplanted into Midwestern America. Church holidays were celebrated in much the same way that they were in Europe. Easter meant that fasting during Lent and extra-long church services would be required for everyone, including us kids. The priests from the church, along with the precinct committeeman, were like the village elders. Both were, in my family, despised behind their backs but accepted as facts of life to be acknowledged and rewarded with contributions or votes, sometimes both.

There was one small grocery store on our block, three bars, a funeral home, a bakery, sausage shop, a butcher shop, a fish market, a vegetable store, a pharmacy or Apteka, and a hot dog stand. Shopping would be a trek from one store to the next getting fresh goods at each place. For holidays such as Easter, special sausages, meats, breads, horseradish, and eggs were taken to the church for blessings. The lines at the shops would start at six in the morning. If you were not early, there would be nothing to take to church. If that happened, the kids that didn't get anything could expect a beating from their parents. Shopping for holidays was very competitive.

Everyone living near us came to America to escape from the oppression of the old country or the ravages of the war that had just ended.

3

They were in America to start a new life and were working to improve themselves, raise their children, and become Americans. Living in a Polish neighborhood was just a place they used as a starting point for their journey to a new and better life than the one they had fled in Europe. While the pull of the old country along with the family that remained there, and the inability to speak English, slowed them down, they expected their children to quickly learn the new ways and to move on in the future.

The old people in the neighborhood only spoke Polish, parents spoke Polish and some English, while the kids spoke both equally well. You spoke Polish to your grandparents, in some stores, and listened when your parents spoke in Polish about things that you were not supposed to know about. Church services and some parochial schools were taught only in Polish, German, or Ukrainian, depending on which side of Milwaukee Avenue you lived.

Parents made sure their children went to church school, as they did not trust public education. But as the priests and nuns continually focused only on the needs of the church, holidays, and collecting funds, students started going to the public schools. The public schools forced English to be used rather than native languages and those kids started speaking better English than those attending parochial ones. For me it was joining the YMCA that caused a break with Polish church schools.

"I want to go to the Y after school," I told my mother.

She told me the priest said that Catholics could not go there, so I asked my dad. He talked to the priest about it one day, and the priest told him that we should pray rather than play after school. Apparently the priest then told him that you could be excommunicated from the Catholic Church for joining a Christian organization. He came home so mad that he told me, "You are changing schools tomorrow, and in the afternoon, you can join the Y."

The next day he enrolled me in a German school, St. Boniface, that taught classes in English and had church services in Latin rather than Polish. It was across Milwaukee Avenue, about six blocks away. That same day I joined the Y. Technically the Division Street YMCA was outside of the neighborhood on the west side of Ashland Avenue, but just across the line. It was great!

What went on in the outside world did not penetrate our neighborhood directly until the Korean War started. A few of the older brothers of my friends enlisted in the Army, and we started collecting Korean War trading cards.

"I'll trade you a MIG for a Sabre jet," or, "How about a Pork Chop Hill (Hill 225) for a Hill 109 (Pusan)?" we would yell on the school playground.

"How about if we just toss for them instead?" Bobbie always suggested. He was the best pitcher in the school. He could pitch or toss his cards onto the window ledge almost every time and win all of the cards that had piled up on the sidewalk below. It was like a craps table that let you win whatever all the other players had thrown but had not won. Bobbie would go home with all the cards almost every time we played. We had to chew lots of Topps gum to get enough trading cards to try beating him.

He lived across Milwaukee Avenue and turned out to be one of our first lessons in believing our parents about not trusting people outside of the neighborhood. My parents said, "He's Lithuanian; you should have expected to be cheated."

We did not have to venture very far outside the neighborhood to find everything we needed, but trips to downtown Chicago on the EL were a special treat. Stores like Marshall Field's and Carson Pirie & Scott brought the world to Chicago. At Christmas, a visit to their windows or the toy department was like going to a fairyland. It was just about a half-hour from home but worlds apart. These visits did not happen very often but for me, they were like visits to a foreign country, even though my mother worked for Field's. My dad also worked in the loop, so it was nothing special for him either. But it sure was for me.

In some ways our family was a bit unusual for the neighborhood, as we moved there from Florida, not Warsaw. We were there because my father's business went bankrupt and he was starting over and had to move in with my mother's family. It was not a happy time for them but they said that they were working hard to get back on their feet, buy a house, and move out of the neighborhood. It was not so bad for me living in my grandmother's buildings with aunts, uncles, and their kids. We always had fun together.

The very first trip I can remember taking without my parents was in the summer of 1948 to the Division Street YMCA's, Camp Channing. I was eight years old. Before then I remember only bits and pieces of trips to and from Florida on the train and cross-country driving trips on Route 66 from Chicago to San Diego and back. I saw that there were lots of other ways to live but, in our neighborhood, there was only one.

Camp was one of the things that played a role in getting me out of thinking just about neighborhood and only doing things in it. The kids at Camp Channing came from many of the neighborhoods around us. I was the only one from my block that went to the camp so playing with all the others seemed like the normal thing to do. Even at the Y itself, very few kids from my neighborhood came to swimming and gym classes. I guess their parents believed what the priests said about the Y being an evil place; if they were right, I guess I missed the evil part.

Everyone spoke English there, all the time. No foreign languages were allowed. It was "Be American, Speak English" regardless of whatever you spoke at home. The kids didn't mind.

Uncle Stanley

We were living in a small town in central Florida in the years right after the war, and the Seaboard Limited train came roaring through town twice a day: once in the late morning going to Miami and the return trip, about dinner time, going to New York. You could almost tell time by it.

We lived in a boarding house since my dad had opened a drug store and we couldn't afford a house. My mom was sick a lot and once she tried to kill herself—at least that is what they told my sister and me. We thought she was just lonely being away from her family in Chicago, but what did we really know? It was hard for my dad to make the store work. He was a Yankee in a small Southern town, and my mother had asked her cousin to come with her to work in the store. I think her name was Connie and she had a boyfriend, Bill, who had a gray pickup truck. He gave us rides to school once in a while. It was really cold riding in the back, but he said it was good for us. He also liked to catch snakes. Connie was described as scatterbrained or "loose," depending who was telling the story.

We had lots of coral snakes, water moccasins, timber rattlers, alligators, and snapping turtles in the small lake across the street from our house. Bill was always catching different ones to show us. We heard that he also sold them for their skins. We weren't sure what you did with their skins, but I guess somebody wanted them for something.

We hoped that that Bill would catch the alligator that bit off little Bobby Jackson's right arm while he was swimming in Lake Weir, but he didn't. Bobby never was quite right after that, but Bill thought it was kind of funny.

One evening after we had been there a while, my mother had what they called a "nervous breakdown," and we had to stay in another room

7

for a few days. The next thing that I remember, I was getting on the train going to Chicago.

Getting to my grandmother's house in Chicago took a few days, and it was hot when we got there. It was really different from Florida, where I had been called either a Yankee or a cracker, depending on who was talking to me. At my grandmother's house, everyone spoke Polish and people were called by their Polish names. The radio stations were Polish, the newspapers, the church services, the store clerks; everyone and everything was Polish. In fact, my grandmother never did speak very much English.

My father eventually arrived back in Chicago after he sold the store in Florida. From what my sister and I could learn, my parents were telling my grandmother and my Aunt Mary, that Connie, who was supposed to help my mom out, was stealing from the store. She and Bill took so much money that the store went bankrupt. I learned that we were something called "broke." That's why we were living in an apartment in my grandmother's house.

House isn't quite the correct word; it was more like a pair of two-story houses on a corner lot. There was no grass and not a tree on the block. Except for the concrete landing outside the basement windows, there was no place to play except on the sidewalk or in the street.

My grandmother's two wooden houses originally did not have indoor plumbing and still did not have hot water when we moved there, but we did have toilets in each apartment.. They were installed only the year before; just after wartime rationing was lifted. My Uncle Stanley put them in.

In its early days, Chicago had some unique ways of building houses. In my grandmother's case, it meant that a two-story house actually had three floors, as the basement was always built a few feet below ground level and the first floor was about six feet above the level of the street. This provided enough space so that toilets could be under the street and would empty directly into the city sewer system.

Most of the houses on our block were built more or less alike using the same system for toilets. We were lucky, as many of the houses still used the under-the-street toilets. "Joe Pod Sidewalk Yem" (an under the sidewalk Joe) was a term we used when picking on kids we didn't like

8

in the neighborhood. Nothing was lower than that, except being called a DP for acting stupid.

DPs were WWII refugees, "Displaced Persons." Some with tattoos, some without, but most of them did not speak English. Some wanted to keep their old ways in our neighborhood, others were following the "Be American, Speak English" approach of my parents. We played with both kinds.

My Uncle Stanley lived in the basement of my grandmother's house. My Aunt Mary, her husband, Joe, and their three kids, Betty, Bonnie, and Ken, lived on the first floor of the back house, and we lived on the second floor. My grandmother and her blind "sister" Josie lived on the top floor of the front building, and two really old ladies from Poland lived on the first floor.

Stanley was supposed to take care of the buildings when anything went wrong. The problem with this arrangement was that Stanley was, we were told, "not right in the head." Others in the neighborhood said he was a drunk, some said he was "nuts," while others said he was both. I really didn't know what any of those words meant, so to me he was just my really old-looking uncle who lived in the smelly and dirty basement.

My grandmother told us that Stanley was in the war and was a combat engineer. He was captured by the Japanese in someplace called New Guinea and had been a Prisoner of War for about two years. I looked in a really cool book called a *History of World War II* (in pictures) and saw that it was all jungle where he was captured. When he was released from the camp, he weighed about eighty pounds, had elephantiasis, malaria, jungle fever, parasites, and several wounds that had been untreated. My mom said that's why he drank a lot. It seemed that lots of guys in our neighborhood must have been there with him because they all drank a lot.

DPs and some POWs were actually common in our neighborhood, but most of them were from Europe and had tattooed numbers on the arms. They did not act like my uncle. He was different from the other guys that drank and got drunk. He taught me lots of stuff, most of which my mother was not too happy about. He was a great artist. He could draw anything with just a small pencil: portraits of Jesus that looked just like him, dogs, cats, Betty Grable (whoever she was), and lots of naked women with big breasts. Mom was especially not pleased with these drawings.

According to both my mom and grandmother, most of the time Stanley was sleeping it off, getting drunk so he could sleep it off, or screaming in his sleep and shouting at everyone, especially my grandmother. I learned lots of good words to tell my friends, as his language was, as my mother described it, very "colorful." My friends said he was swearing. Uncle Stanley was really good at bad swearing and cursing.

My friends and I made some distinctions about swearing and cursing. Swearing was really only using bad words. Cursing was another matter altogether; you could go to hell for doing it. Cursing was what Uncle Stanley mostly did with my grandmother and swearing was what he mostly did with everyone else. He did not like my grandmother saying "she never should have had him," whatever that meant, and always cursed at her when she said it.

He was the best at making model aircraft out of balsa wood and tissue paper. He had dozens of them all over his apartment: Hellcats, Avengers, B-29s, P-51s, B-32, and PBY 2s all painted and looking real enough to fly away. He was a real artist. He even had a great picture he drew of the Thinker (he said it was a Roman statue) in his toilet that said, "Some people sit and think, others just shit and stink." Directly over the toilet was a sign that said, "Gentlemen, in your hand lies the future of this country." That one I did not understand.

You never knew what Uncle Stanley was going to do or say. I once told him that I wanted to be a pilot and he got very angry and crushed most of the models he had built while screaming at me: "The world does not need any more Goddamn pilots!" At other times he could also be very gentle and kind.

The first Christmas we were living in Chicago it was bitterly cold. I had asked Santa for a puppy and sure enough, a very, very small one turned up in my Christmas stocking. He was a black bundle of fur that my cousins from downstairs and I played with all Christmas day. My mom said it was from Uncle Stanley. At the end of the day, my cousins went back home and gave me back the puppy. It did not seem to be acting right, so I asked my dad about it and he said something was wrong with its back legs. "Were you squeezing it too tight?" my dad asked.

"No," I said. "Well you should ask your uncle Stanley if he knows what's wrong."

I took the dog—it didn't even have a name yet—down to Stanley and told him what had happened. He was somewhere between drunk and not so drunk when I got there but listened intently. He then picked the dog from my hands and placed it on the table and tried to see if it could stand; it could not. He did a few more tests on the whimpering animal and told me that someone had squeezed it too tightly and had broken its back. I said that we didn't squeeze it and didn't know what happened, as we would never hurt it.

He picked the dog up by its back legs, spun it around, and smashed its head against the floor. It made a slight thud. He turned to me and said, "No more fucking dogs for you until you know how to take care of them. Go home!" He picked up a bottle of beer and went back into his bedroom. I stood there crying, looking at the pile of crumpled fur and then ran back upstairs.

I stayed away from Stanley as much as I could after that. I didn't know if he was right about my not knowing how to take care of an animal, but we never had another dog or cat after that. It was OK because my mother was allergic to just about everything, including pets.

We eventually saved enough money to buy a home of our own and moved away from my grandmother's house. We saw Stanley once in a while at holidays after that, but we were never again close. About five years later when I was about fourteen years old and was working in a pharmacy near our old neighborhood, I saw him walking alone across Chicago Avenue. He looked really good, like he was almost normal. But by the time I could get out of the store to cross the street, he had disappeared. I never saw him again.

Several years later, I read a story in one of the Chicago newspapers about three men who died after drinking tainted alcohol. It happened at a SRO (single room occupancy) hotel, what most people would call a flophouse, on Maxwell Street. We called that area "Skid Row." One of the names was Stanley Gongola: Uncle Stanley. The interesting thing that came from the article was that my Aunt Ellen sued the hotel and whiskey manufacturer for his death. It was so typical of our family. She had never had anything to do with him while he was alive, but she was now trying to profit from his death. I'm sure he would enjoy the irony.

11

I can still remember looking at the bayonet scar running down Uncle Stanley's left arm, the draining sores on his legs, and the sweaty sheets after he would wake from a malaria-induced sleep thinking that if he had run faster those things would not have happened to him.

I was lucky while I was in the Army and was never captured. I never did get the pin-up girl tattoo on my arm like his, nor did I learn to drink like the guys in my old neighborhood.

Stanley was a combination of the crazy uncle you kept locked away in the basement, the adventurer who was treated badly by fate, and the lost spirit trapped in the body of an addict. He was one of a kind in my life, not someone I wanted to emulate but someone who deserved better.

Maybe he found what he was looking for in the bottle his group of friends passed around the day the bad liquor killed them. I certainly hope so.

Easter

Shopping during Holy Week in our neighborhood for Easter food was like playing street stickball. Old ladies would cut in line and dare you to say something to them. Otherwise nice kids would push in front of you to get a lower number. Everyone had to have everything so they could get the sausages cooked, eggs dyed, horseradish grated, and butter lambs and rye bread into baskets to be blessed on Holy Saturday. God help the kid or buscia who dropped a basket or was late to church for the blessing.

"Run ahead and get in line," my mother said as she put on her coat.

Off I went at full speed and ran the three blocks to Division Street. I bounced up the five stairs to the meat market and grabbed a green number sixteen from the wall. I counted only five old ladies waiting around. The clock over the butcher block showed it was only 8:15.

Another ten old ladies and a few kids from school soon crowded into the store waiting for their number to be called. My mother and grandmother walked in just as number fifteen was being called. I gave them the number and ran out of the store.

My real job for the morning was to get to the bakery and buy the stuff for Easter. "Do you remember what you're supposed to get?" she asked before we left the house.

"Yeah."

"So tell me," she said, grabbing her purse.

"OK, four loaves of round rye with the purple-and-white crosses, dozen and a half Pączki with jelly, cream, prune, and apple, two honey babkas, and a dozen crullers. Aunt Mary wanted three rye, one white sliced, and half a dozen plain donuts."

"Right. Don't let them give you any old ones from yesterday. Check everything they put in the bags. Count your change."

"Yeah, yeah, I know."

"Well just make sure you get everything. There are no second chances today."

I was supposed to get back home to help Aunt Mary finish making the Pierogi. We couldn't start coloring the Easter eggs until we finished with the mess of making them. She was making enough sauerkraut, potato, cheese, and some with prunes for everyone in the family.

"The water's boiling," I told her.

"Well start putting them in the pot so we can get finished. Get about a dozen at a time in there. They'll float when they're done," she coaxed, brushing the loose stands of hair from her face. "I can't help you right now. I got to finish setting Josie's hair."

It took me about an hour to finish them. They would be fried on Easter Sunday. She now had a real Frigidaire, not the old icebox, so stuff would not spoil like last year when she ran out of ice before the ice wagon arrived.

It was almost noon and work was supposed to stop between noon and three o'clock, while Jesus was hanging on the cross. Coloring eggs was supposed to be a quiet thing to do, but I guess my cousins were not told about the quiet part. They yelled and carried on until Aunt Mary gave each one of them a good smack on the head with her hand and said, "Shut up. Jesus is dying for you right now, and you don't deserve it!"

Eggs were a mess to color. Aunt Mary had set up eight cups with vinegar water and color drops for us to use. Everything was on top of thick layers of newspapers so that the coloring would not stain the wooden kitchen table. It was already stained from years before of egg coloring, but maybe this year everyone would be more careful. It didn't work.

"Look out, Ken," Bonnie screeched, just as he tipped over the blue dye cup and spilled it all over the newspapers.

"What?" he asked.

"You just spilled," she said.

"No, I didn't."

"Mom, Kenny's spilling again," she yelled louder.

The radio in the living room went off at noon but would begin Polish services again from Holy Trinity Church at 3:00 o'clock. Aunt Mary came storming into the kitchen and wacked each of us and told us to be quiet.

"Clean up that mess before it stains," she said, walking back into her room.

The table now had some blue added to the other faded colors under the matted papers.

It took about another hour to finish and get the eggs set onto drying racks before they went into the Frigidaire.

Early the next morning the final shopping was done and baskets were prepared to carry to Holy Trinity Church for the blessing. We had three large baskets: one from my grandmother, one from Aunt Mary, and ours.

It looked like a line of black ants moving toward the church before each blessing. Hundreds of black babushkas carrying round or oblong wicker baskets covered in white linen moved into the church and then back out a few minutes later. It went on all morning.

Only blessed food could be served on Easter. If you didn't get to the store on time or get everything on the list, something was going to be missing from Easter breakfast.

The rest of Holy Saturday was usually spent doing final shopping for new clothes for Easter Sunday. My Mom, sister, and I walked to the Buster Brown store on Milwaukee Avenue where I got fitted for new shoes. They had one of those X-ray machines that showed how well your feet fit into the shoes. You could see your toes wiggling inside while they were checking the size. I got a pair of black dress ones.

All my other clothes came from the store where my mom worked. I didn't have to spend time walking all over like she and my sister did trying stuff on. They let me carry my shoes home alone while they looked for dresses and hats for Easter. It was only about eight blocks from the store to our house. I was almost to our street when four older boys came out of the alley across from the hot dog stand and stopped me.

"What ya got there?" asked the tallest.

"What?" I answered.

"What's in the bag, stupid?"

"Shoes."

"What kind of shoes?"

"Buster Brown."

"I got shoes, you got shoes, everybody's got to have shoes," he sang, "but there's only one kind of shoe for me."

"Good ole Buster Brown," the rest of them answered.

"You really got Buster Browns in there?" the short one asked.

I nodded.

"Let me see," he said.

I handed him the bag. He pulled the box out and looked at the size. He smiled.

"Thanks kid, you saved me a trip to the store."

"Why?" I stammered

"Because these are my size. That's why."

"You can't have them; they're mine."

"Listen kid, we can take you back in the alley and cut you up. Which do you want, these shoes or all of your fingers?" the older one said, pulling out a switchblade knife.

I shivered and said nothing.

"Thanks, kid," they said, walking away and laughing.

The old one turned around from the alley and said, "Hey kid, tell anybody and I'll come back to your house and pluck your magic twanger off. Got it?"

I nodded. They walked away laughing and slapping each other on the back.

Shaking, I slowly went home to wait for my mom to return. When she did, I told her what happened and she slapped me for getting caught by the boys.

She calmed down and asked, "Are they from the neighborhood?"

"No."

"Ever seen them before?"

"No."

"Would you recognize them if you saw them again?"

"Maybe."

When my dad got home, we told him what happened. He went down stairs to talk with Uncle Joe.

Joe said that he knew the father of one of those guys from work. He said the son hung out with a bunch of toughs that lived over near North Avenue and Ashland.

"They cut up a few kids just for fun. They roam around the city looking for trouble all the time. Don't fool around with them."

It was too late to get new shoes, so I polished up the old ones. We didn't have the money to buy another pair anyway, even if the store was still open.

We decided to go to seven o'clock Mass on Easter morning so my old shoes would not be noticed as much. I was especially thankful that the boys only took my shoes and didn't cut me up. It was pretty good to have had Jesus save me from them. Nobody seemed to notice that my shoes were old.

After Mass we ate all the stuff from the blessed basket for breakfast. Kielbasa, rye bread with a purple-and-white cross on it, butter lamb, horseradish, soup made from sausage and horseradish, hard boiled eggs, Pierogi, and hot cross buns. We all knew there would be a lamb roast for dinner but ate like pigs anyway.

We finished eating early and decided to try getting in to see *The Robe* playing in the loop for the 11:30 showing. We made it. It was perfect for Easter and we saw it in widescreen Cinemascope.

It was about three o'clock when we got home to make dinner. The lamb roast was Greek style with lots of lemon and garlic, popovers, green beans, and mashed potatoes. My dad had a few drinks of Jim Beam while it was cooking. He never drank much, but I guess it was OK to do on holidays.

We didn't eat until late, so my sister and I watched television until almost six o'clock. My parents had bought a big TV set so that we would not have to go out of the house to play. They thought it was safer for us to be at home rather than playing on the streets. I thought it was great to watch when I was tired after playing outside.

It had been pretty cold all weekend and it seemed like the temperature had dropped even more when I went downstairs in just my shirt to take out the garbage after dinner. My Uncle Stanley was coming out of his basement apartment when I was walking across the gangway from the garbage cans. He put up his hand to stop me.

"Joe told me about those guys."

"Yeah, they were pretty scary."

"Well, don't worry about them anymore."

"Why not, they're still around. The one even said he knew where I lived."

"They won't be causing anyone trouble."

"Why not?"

"They picked the wrong guy over on Paulina. He was home for Easter from the Marines. He was just back from Korea."

"What happened?"

"He's small and looks really young. They tried holding him up with a knife. He broke one guy's arm, crushed a windpipe, and another guy won't ever walk right again. One ran away."

"Gee, when did that happen?"

"Friday night, about seven thirty. The kid came in the Dew Drop for a shot and a beer right after he cleaned up the street with them."

"Did the police arrest him?"

"Hell no, the cops hauled that trash to county. Told the docs the boys got into a fight. Never did find the other guys. The dicks did come to the bar though. Bought the kid a beer. Saved them lots of paperwork. Told him to enjoy his leave and think about joining the force when he gets out."

"Wow!" was all I could say.

"Trash like that don't deserve to be on the streets. Good riddance, should have killed all of them, would have saved everyone lots of time and money. You can bet they'll think twice before picking on anyone again, if they ever have a next time."

"Thanks, I was really worried they might come and hurt me next time, just for fun."

"Well, I seen guys like that in the jungle. Lots of talk but they usually end up with a bullet in their back for running away. Fucking punks."

I shivered and said, "Goodnight, thanks again for telling me."

"Sure kid, anytime. Stay out of trouble. It'll come looking for you," he said with a very sad look on his weather-beaten, scarred up face.

He turned away, walked up the steps to the street, and turned in the direction of the corner bar. I went back upstairs to warm up and to stop thinking about that knife shining in the street lamp.

Turning Over a New Leaf

My mother and father yelled at each other lots after we moved to my grandmother's house from Florida. My dad was upset that Mom's cousin Connie had taken money from their store and made it go bankrupt. He did not want to live with Mom's family; people might think we were on welfare because of what happened with the drug store.

Dad had lots of friends in Chicago from before he married Mom. They helped him buy a small grocery store near someplace called Palmer Square. He ran the store for a while then said we all needed to be there because it took too long to drive back and forth. We moved again.

"You're going to St. Sylvester's starting next week," my mom told me. "I talked to the priest at Holy Trinity and they're sending your report card over to the Sisters. It's a good school, and it's in English."

"Polish, English; it's all the same. I'll have to make new friends again," I wailed.

"Too bad, we can't stay here. Your father wants another business, so we're moving."

"I like it here. My cousins are here."

"We're moving. That's it. Stop crying about it; you're giving me a headache."

We moved into the apartment behind Dad's grocery store on a Sunday. My dad had to run the store all the other days, so all of us carried stuff to the car and we drove over to our new house. It already had furniture, so we just put our clothes in drawers. We could just walk across the hall to the store if we needed something to eat. There were even cases of Mission Bell orange soda bottles stacked outside our door.

Maybe this won't be so bad.

School was about eight blocks away. My dad took me the first morning before the store opened. The principal welcomed me and took me right to church where morning Mass was going on.

Sister Mary Michael had me stand in front of the class and introduce myself.

"My name is," I started as I put my book bag on the edge of the front desk. I looked around at all the new faces, missed the desk, and everything, including my lunch, spilled on the floor.

The room exploded in laughter, my faced turned red. Sister said, "Pick up your things quickly. Go sit down."

The kids dropped things off their desks all morning copying me. Sister finally told the class, "Stop dropping things or no recess today."

———

"Liver sausage and ketchup sandwich? Yuck!" the skinny kid sitting behind me said, looking over my shoulder at lunch.

"It's good, want to try it?" I said, handing him half.

"Uh uh, you eat those all the time?"

"Sure, they're good. What're you eating?"

"Peanut butter and grape jelly."

"Want to trade?"

"No way, liver sausage is terrible."

"Ever try it?"

"No, but it looks bad," he said way too loud. Some of the other kids heard him and came over to look.

"That looks bad. That looks bad," they chanted until Sister Mary Michael looked up and noticed the fuss going on at my desk.

She wacked the desk with her yardstick and everyone quieted down. She pointed and waved me to her desk.

"Is this why you transferred to St. Sylvester's, because you cause trouble?"

"No, Sister." I shook my head.

"It had better not be or you won't be here very long either. Now go sit down and keep out of trouble."

I nodded and slouched back to my desk toward the back of the classroom.

The day could not have ended soon enough. The three o'clock bell sounded and everyone stood up, recited a prayer, and filed for the door.

Sister stopped me and asked, "Are you from California?" I said I had been there once, so she pulled me out of one line going down the stairs and put me in another. We filed out of the building, across the schoolyard, and into the street where kids scattered in every direction. I just stood there. I had no idea where I was.

About ten minutes later, they locked the gates to the school and I stood on the street looking around for the way home. It was not here.

My father was on the other side of the school, where he had dropped me off in the morning, patiently waiting for me. When I didn't show up, he went inside and talked to the nuns about where I was. They tracked down Sister Mary Michael, who told them I said I lived on California Street and that she put me in that exit line.

The principal, Sister Mary Michael, and my father all walked from the school to the back gate.

"Why did you tell me you lived on California?" Sr. Mary Michael demanded, grabbing at me.

"I thought you asked if I had ever been to California," I said, twisting away from her grasp.

My father grabbed her arm. "Don't do that!" he said.

The principal, moving between them, said softly, "I think everyone needs to calm down."

"If he does something wrong, I'll take care of it at home. Your nuns will not touch him; I'll do it."

"Now just a minute," the principal began.

"No, if he does wrong, send a note, call me; it's my job, not yours, to lay a hand on him."

"If he misbehaves, I will discipline him," Sister Mary Michael said.

"Talk to him, send him to the principle, but do not touch him."

"That's not how we do it here. If they misbehave, we will slap them or whack them with a ruler, or make them stay after school and wash blackboards."

21

"If you hit him ever again, I'll come here and do the same thing to you. I will make the discipline in my family."

The principle raised her hands. "I think we have all gotten off on the wrong foot today. We had some misunderstandings that will not be repeated. Isn't that right, Sister?" she said, nodding to Sister Mary Michael.

"Ah, yes, Sister, that's right," she said nodding and lowering her head.

"Good, now that that's settled, let's get everybody back home now, shall we?"

My father took me by the arm and we all walked back through the school and out the building on the Palmer Square side. He nodded to them and tightened his grip on my arm. We walked toward the park and home.

We didn't talk about what happened but late that night, I heard him yelling at my mom about me. He was not happy about something.

———

There were lots of kids to play with in the neighborhood. Sometimes they came over and played in the hallway behind the store. My dad let us listen to the radio after school. Straight Arrow, Bobby Benson and the B-Bar-B Riders, and Sargent Preston of the Yukon were all on before dinner.

"I'm going to get an inch of land in the Yukon," I told my mom.

"What land? Where? What are you talking about?"

"From Sgt. Preston, they're giving it away. Tell Dad he has to sell Quaker Puffed Wheat so I can get some in the boxes."

"You get land with the cereal?"

"Yep, we need to get some in the store."

"I'll talk to him about it."

I gave her a hug and ran out to tell the other kids I was going to get some land.

We had a big mulberry tree down the block that was really messy, dropping berries all over the street and sidewalk. They stained our shoes, pants, and hands when we touched them. Since they were next to two big empty lots where we played jungle, we were always dirty.

"Here, use my old BB gun," Mike said, handing me his pump-action rifle. "It doesn't really work anymore, so you can just use it as a fake one."

"Great," I said, trying to cock it. "Let's go kill some Japs!" The pump action just slid back and forth but never seemed to have any pressure in it. When it was cocked, it kind of looked like a tommy gun, so that's the way I carried it in the jungle. My left hand gripped the "V" were the pump action bent and the right was on the trigger, just like what they showed in the war movies. I got to play a Marine trying to capture a Jap pillbox. I rushed up to it spraying bullets all over the defenders when the pump action suddenly snapped forward catching my hand.

I screamed and tried to drop the gun. It would not fall. It was clamped onto the skin between my thumb and first finger and was just hanging there with blood running down my hand and arm.

Mike ran the block to my dad's store and told him what happened. I sat on the ground, crying and bleeding. Dad ran with Mike to where I was sitting and looked at the gun dangling from my bloody hand. He gripped the pump action and pushed it open. It fell off my hand and the blood gushed out. "Here," he said, "push this rag on the cut real hard." I did and the bleeding slowed down. He put his arm around me and walked me home. We put some ice on it from the ice cream cooler and waited till Mom came home.

"Twenty stitches," the old doctor said as he was wrapping up my hand. "Come back in ten days, and we'll take um out. Don't get your hand wet between now and then." He had numbed my hand so I didn't feel anything but tired. I fell asleep in the car going home. I guess my dad carried me to bed because it was morning the next thing I knew.

"Be careful at school today," my mother said. "I'll write a note to the nuns about what happened."

She didn't have to. All the kids knew that the Japs got me the day before and I had to go with the medics. It felt good to be a hero, even for only one morning. After a while, trying to do schoolwork with only one good hand was not so much fun. Sister Mary Michael was not pleased. Again I had to have special attention. She had me answer extra questions, work additional math problems, and she graded my homework with a really sharp pencil. A few days later, she caught me talking at

23

morning Mass and pulled me out of the pew by my ear. She sent me to the principal's office.

About an hour later, my dad was sitting next to me across the desk from Sister Mary Michael and the principal. "He's disruptive, always talking in church, does not have his assignments done properly. He is a bad influence walking around here with his hand bandaged up from war games. You should be ashamed of what he's doing at school," Sister Mary Michael said to my father, while pointing at me.

My father kept nodding his head in agreement with whatever she was saying until she said, "If he doesn't change, and change quickly, I will have no alternative but to expel him from St. Sylvester's for being a troublemaker and disruptive."

"I agree," he said. I couldn't believe he was agreeing with her. The Sisters nodded.

He continued, "I've been too lenient with him. He is going to change. In fact he will turn over a new leaf starting today."

They nodded more vigorously.

He turned to me. "Tell them you will turn over a new leaf today."

"Who? What?" I stammered.

He grabbed my arm hard. "Tell them you will turn over a new leaf starting today."

"OK," I told him.

I turned, looked at Sister Mary Michael, and said, "I'll turn over a new leaf starting today."

They nodded solemnly to both of us. "See that you do," said the principal. Sister Mary Michael bobbed her head and left the office.

"I think you should beat him when you get home; he has the devil in him," she said.

My dad got up and said, "I'll make sure he gets what's coming to him when we get home."

He turned to me and said, "Tell her you're sorry for causing all this trouble."

I did and we walked out of the small, hot, and stuffy office.

My dad didn't say much on the eight-block walk home. "Can I ask you a question?" I said.

"Yes."

"Where do I get the new leaves I'm supposed to turn over, and then what do I do with them?" I asked.

He burst out laughing.

"You had no idea what they were talking about, did you?"

"No, sir. I didn't. I just don't understand what those leaves they kept talking about are supposed to do to make me behave better."

We didn't say anything else till we got back home.

When we got there, he told me to go to my room and he would come in when he figured out what to do with me.

About ten minutes later, he walked in and gave me a frozen drumstick ice cream. "Eat it! We'll talk about the leaves some other time. Just don't get the nuns mad at you anymore this year. You only have another month before summer. Maybe next year you'll have a better teacher."

I hoped he was right. One that wasn't so interested in leaves.

The Fourth of July

You could hear explosions all over the neighborhood. At night Roman candles streaked through the streets with red fireballs bouncing off cars and roofs. Snakes, sparklers, cherry bombs, two-inchers, fountains, Roman candles, and ladyfingers were all over the place.

My mom wouldn't let me have anything but snakes and some sparklers.

"You'll lose your fingers or maybe an eye with those things," she yelled out the gangway window.

"But everyone has them; even Kenney and Bonnie can have them," I whined. They were my cousins who lived downstairs.

"I don't care what your Aunt Mary lets them do. You're not touching any of those things. They're dangerous."

"Well, you're supposed to make noise on the fourth, aren't you?"

"Let someone else make it; I won't have you doing it. That's final. Keep crying about it and you won't even have sparklers; they're bad enough." Her head went back inside the curtains.

It was a few days before the fourth, and already one kid on the next block lost two fingers on his left hand from a cherry bomb. He bet his friends that he could hold it in his hand until just before it exploded and then throw it away. The fuse burned faster than he thought. He was just letting it go when it blew up. His friends told us that the two middle fingers on his right hand looked like shredded bloody chicken feet when they called his mom to get him. He was still in the hospital.

Kasz was there when it happened and told me, "He held it way too long. He was dumb."

"Well, it doesn't make any difference. My mom won't let me have any fireworks anyway."

"I've got some ladyfingers. You can have a few," he offered.

"Thanks. My cousins have lots too. They let me light some of theirs with my punk. My Uncle Joe brings bags of stuff home from work. He said some guy buys it at Lake Geneva and sells it from his truck next to the factory over on Clybourn. He sets off the big stuff; they just get the small ones."

"Your mom lets you have punks?" he asked with a funny look on his face.

"Sure, why not, they don't blow up or anything. I can light snakes with them too, but I need matches for the sparklers."

"Can I have a few punks? I'll let you watch me blow up ants with ladyfingers over by the viaduct on Division. There's some big ant hills over there now."

"OK, that sounds like fun."

There were no streets that went very far in our neighborhood so the cars usually went slow until they got to Paulina Street. We played street baseball, roller-skated, used scooters that we made from old wooden fruit boxes, and ran all over without worrying about traffic. The only time we had to be cautious was when a delivery truck barreled down the street or when a horse and wagon came through selling stuff. That changed on July third!

A game of street baseball was on when a 1948 Desoto came roaring around the corner from Troop Street and into the middle of the game right in front of my house. Little Billy Novak couldn't get all the way out of the street. The car swerved, but his right arm got caught in the door handle and he was dragged down the block toward the bar on the corner. We ran after them.

The car started going faster and Billy fell off the door and into the street between the bar and the grocery store across from it.

We all ran over to where he was. One of the men from the bar was already next to Billy by the time we got there. There was blood all over the place. The man pulled off his undershirt and was holding it over Billy's shoulder trying to stop the bleeding. One of the other men went into the bar to call an ambulance. He came out a few minutes later with a bottle of clear liquor and some towels from the bar. He poured the liquor on the towels and put them over where Billy was bleeding. Billy screamed like a wild animal and then passed out.

About ten minutes later, the police and a fire ambulance got there. Billy was still passed out, and the man was still pressing the towels over his shoulder. When the ambulance guys moved the towel, we could see that Billy's arm was not there; it had been torn off by the car. The guys in the bar had been in the army and knew what to do; otherwise, Billy would have bled to death in the street.

It was pretty quiet on our block for the rest of the day. Some of the kids puked, others were crying. All of us were afraid to go back into the street. The moms who were home called their kids inside for the rest of the afternoon; nobody wanted to play anyways.

That night my mom said that the car had crashed into a light pole on Division and Western. The police found Billy's arm still in the door handle. Both guys were drunk.

———

"Yo, Dickie!" came the yell even before I was out of bed. "Come out and play!" Kasz and Wally were in front of my house yelling from the street.

"Yo!" they yelled again.

I looked out the open window and waved to show that I was awake and put up five fingers.

"See you in five," Kasz yelled.

I nodded.

A slice of white bread, grape jelly, and some milk took three minutes; sneakers, shirt, and shorts another two. Then I was out the door, down the stairs, and into the street. Everyone else at home was still sleeping.

"What took you so long?" they said.

I just looked at him.

"Where we going?" I asked.

"Don't know. It was too hot to sleep, so I got Kasz up," said Wally.

"Yeah, what can we do now?"

"Everything's closed today, and I'm sure not going to Mass this morning," Kasz answered.

"Anybody got any money?" I asked and checked my pockets. "I got a dime."

Everyone checked and we ended up with a quarter between us.

"We could go to the bakery and get some donuts and split a milk?" I suggested.

We all started running over to Division Street.

"Holy cow," said Wally. "The lines out the door already."

Kasz ran ahead of us to get a green number tag. He came back down the stairs with number thirty-nine.

"Everybody must have the same idea. When it's too hot to sleep, they get donuts," I said.

The streets were steaming. It was really getting hot by the time we got our donuts and walked back to Smerczki's grocery store on our block. Mrs. S gave us three half-pints of milk for the last dime we had.

"Thank you, Mrs. S," we all cheered as she handed us the cold bottles.

"Drink them outside, and bring the empties back. I don't want to go looking for the bottles," she said.

We sat in the shade on the curb next to the store. Not many people were up yet, so it was quiet. It was really hot. The firemen had opened the hydrants early that morning to clean the blood off the street, but nobody wanted to play in the water. The blood was mostly gone, but some spots were still there across the street on the curb.

"I hope Billy is OK," I said.

"Yeah, maybe we should have gone to church this morning to pray for him. He could probably use some help, don't you guys think?"

"Uh huh," said Kasz, munching on his donut, crumbs spreading across the front of his T-shirt.

"He'll be all right. The guys from the bar got to him fast. I don't know if I could stick my hands in someone's blood like that," said Wally.

"It must not be too bad. I saw John Wayne in *Sands of Iwo Jima*, and those guys were doing it all the time," Kasz added.

Wally and I nodded in agreement.

I thought, *Yeah, Billy will be fine in a few days. I sure hope so, but without an arm, I'm not so sure.* I didn't say anything to the guys.

Lizzy, Danuta, and Carol all came out from my cousin Bonnie's flat and started drawing a Sky Blue on the sidewalk. They saw us.

"You want to play? We can beat you!" they started yelling across the street.

"Come on, let's go beat them," Kasz said.

We went back to give our empty bottles to Mrs. S. and then ran the four doors to my house.

"Girls go first," they shouted. They never said stuff quietly.

We played Sky Blue, Hop Scotch, Movie Stars, and jumped rope until my mom called me for lunch. Everybody split up with promises to meet-up later before the fireworks started.

On and off I heard loud explosions from cherry bombs and two-inchers while we were playing with the girls. By the time lunch was over, it sounded like a war was starting on our block. Even during the day, bottle rockets were shooting across the streets, snakes were melting on the sidewalks, and ants were dying by the thousands from ladyfingers blowing up their nests.

The heat seemed to bring more people outside than normal; they sat on their front stoops and drank beer. My Uncle Joe was out there by noon with his normal Miller High Life bottle, wearing a sleeveless, sweaty undershirt. A large box of fireworks was next to him.

During the summer it does not start to get dark in Chicago until 9:00 o'clock, but red-and-green streaks of fire were shooting across the sky long before then.

"Wow, look at that!" I yelled as gold, red, and blue sparks and stars fell from the smoke-filled clouds over our block.

My parents seemed to have disappeared for the evening; not that they ever spent much time with my mom's sister and her family, or the neighbors. Even my sister was off with friends to somewhere else. I didn't care, though; nothing was better than the fourth on our block.

"Here, light some off," Kasz said, handing me some one-inchers.

"Where did you get them?"

"Your Uncle Joe gave some to Ken, and he gave them to me. They have lots."

We lit a string of them all at one time. It sounded just like a machine gun in the movies.

"Can you ask him for more?"

"I can try."

I watched from the gangway as Kasz went up to my uncle and talked to him. Joe put down his beer, reached into his box, and handed something to Kasz. It took both hands for him to bring it back to where I was hiding.

"Oh, my God," he said. "Look at this stuff!"

While we were sorting out the packages, Uncle Joe got up from the stairs and kind of stumbled down to the street clutching his box. He knocked over a bunch of beer bottles that were next to him. They broke and made a mess when they crashed down onto the concrete next to the basement windows. Aunt Mary was not going to be happy. It looked like he was drunk.

He took out some fountains and Roman candles and shot them off. Next he lit a few starburst rockets that exploded into a splash of red and silver. He then found a big silver-colored box, pulled out its long fuse, and touched his punk to it. He wobbled back behind the Hudson parked in front of the house and waited as the fuse slowly moved toward the box.

The first explosion from the box launched a fiery silver streak into the sky, higher than anything so far on our block. There were two loud reports and some flashes of light really high above our house. It looked like the box moved when the first shot went off. It was now on its side facing the Hudson. It went off again.

"Holy cow!" I managed to yell as I ducked under the street onto the stairs to the toilets below the sidewalk. A ball of fire sped under the Hudson, hit the curb, and went into the air leaving a trail of smoke and red stars. Three very loud explosions shook the neighborhood. I peeked from the stairway and saw that the box was now facing toward the factory and the railroad tracks across the street. Uncle Joe was lying on the sidewalk with his hands over his head moaning.

A final thud came from the silver box and another red streak shot down the street about knee level and struck the raised railroad embankment, bounced back, and hit the grill of the Hudson. Three explosions later the front of the car was wrecked, its windows cracked, and one tire was on fire. Uncle Joe was in tears and shaking so bad that Aunt Mary had to take him into the house.

We all looked at each other and said, "Wow!"

31

"Was that great or what?" Kasz said.

"Amazing!" said Ken

"I wonder what he'll buy for next year," I said.

I could hear Uncle Joe whimpering as I passed their apartment door going up to bed. Aunt Mary was talking softly to him, which was unusual for her, so something really must have been wrong.

Mr. Kozlowski would probably be coming over soon to see about getting his Hudson repaired. I didn't want to be around for that.

Summer Camp

"A hundred bottles of beer on the wall, a hundred bottles of beer, if one of those bottles should happen to fall, ninety-nine bottles of beer on the wall; ninety-nine bottles of beer on the wall," we screamed at the top of our lungs as the two Blue Bird buses pulled away from the front of the Division Street YMCA and started toward Michigan.

We were all still singing "one bottle of beer on the wall" by the time we cleared the loop and were heading toward the state line.

Each bus held about forty campers and five counselors. We would all be together for two weeks playing, learning crafts, swimming, boating, and getting lots of fresh air and good food. A few of the kids had been to the camp last summer and were telling us all about what it was like.

"Get a top bunk," Billy Wojtec warned. "Otherwise you'll always have sand in your bed."

"Yeah," said some kid I'd seen around but didn't know. "You won't get any snakes either."

"Snakes?" several of us shouted. "Are there snakes there?"

"Oh, yeah there are," one of the younger counselors said with a smile. "We had one about four feet long in Cabin Ten last summer." Then he added, "We think they have a nest under the floor. It was only a small blue racer. The big ones can get up to seven feet."

We all just looked at each other and the bus became very quiet.

"Nobody said anything about snakes before we got on the bus," I said to him. He just smiled.

Six hours and a sack lunch later, we pulled into the dirt road leading to Camp Channing. Scott Lake was sparkling through the trees behind the mess hall and the first row of pine log cabins. It took about an hour to get us assigned to cabins, move our suitcases there, and get us changed into swimsuits and down to the lake. The buddy system, swimming rules, and water safety were carefully explained, and then we were turned loose for an hour of free swim. After we dried off, we had an assembly in the mess hall. We met the camp director, Mr. Sven; the head counselor, Mr. Levi; the nurse; and the camp cooks. They gave us all the camp rules and schedules. By the time all the talking was done, it was time for dinner. Boy, was it good!

Lake Scott had a sandy bottom and a spring that kept the water cool, even on hot days. It also had lots of seaweed outside of the swimming area. The lifeguards had to cut the weeds almost every day inside the area between the piers that jutted out into the lake. Both sides of the swim area were thick with weeds that made getting the canoes out into the main part of the lake difficult. Sometimes when someone was particularly disliked, they would be thrown into the weeds rather than the swimming part of the lake. We almost had a kid drown one night when a counselor threw him into the water. He panicked when his feet were caught in the weeds. One of the lifeguards had to jump in and pull him out. Both were sent home the next day: the kid for being a problem camper, and the counselor for getting caught throwing him in.

It was amazing how quickly the routine of camp became second nature to the campers. After a few days, most of us fell into the rhythm of the place and looked forward to mealtime, games, and horsing around. What happened with the Cubs and what would be playing at the Division Theater was important when we were at home, but at camp nobody ever talked about Chicago. It turned out that watching muskrats build a home or squirrels collect nuts was more fun and important than three movies, twenty-five cartoons, and three serials on a Saturday morning in the city.

Some of the counselors thought it was funny to tell ghost stories around the campfire. On the second night, we were sitting around on logs watching the fire burn down when they told the story of "Roberta Mannering."

"Roberta was a farm wife who went crazy and killed her family with an axe, burned down their house, and ran away into the woods screaming," Monty, the counselor, slowly said. "The Mannering farm is just to the south of our camp, and you can still see the burned-out foundation of the house from the road as you drive in."

Every once in a while, a counselor would dress up as Roberta and scare campers going to the latrine building at night to shower. Once Roberta ran screaming into a cabin and grabbed a kid and tried to drag him out the door into the woods. The kid was frightened so badly that he had to be sent home halfway through the session. His parents came to get him. They were not very happy. Roberta did not appear again that summer, and we lost another counselor.

Meals were when songs were sung, prayers said, and all the campers were together. All other times we were only with the kids in their cabins and were in competition with the other cabins for awards that were presented at the end of the session. There were organized sports such as baseball, horseshoes, archery, BB guns, swimming, canoeing, and track and field. There were also night games in the woods, such as flasher, snipe hunting, and whistler that everyone had to play.

When we were not playing games in groups, swimming, boating, and craft skills were waiting to be learned. There was also a bonfire almost every night, and we would sing and tell stories. The first song we learned was "I'm from Camp Channing, Camp Channing. Best camp in the land. Joy on every hand. I'm from Camp Channing…" It echoed around the campfire every night.

We learned about how camp "really worked" on the second day. The main rule was, "If you win games, you get special stuff." First on this list was riding in the Jungle Cruiser. It appeared in camp a few days later. This tired jeep just came back from the repair shop but still didn't sound too good.

"I want to ride in the Jungle Cruiser!" we all yelled as the dark green clunker chugged to a stop by the campfire pit.

"OK, let's see who goes today," Levi shouted as we all waved our arms frantically.

"Me, me, me!" we all kept yelling.

"OK, Billy, Dickie, Gene, and John, get in the back," Levi yelled over the noise of the old engine.

"Yeah!" we shouted as we clambered aboard for the short ride to the beach, "To the beach, to the beach!" we yelled as we bounced over the rutted sand to the shoreline.

Getting to ride in the jungle cruiser was a special treat reserved for campers who had a good score on one of the skills tests. I got aboard because I

35

had moved up from minnow to fish on my swimming test. I'm not sure what the other kids got theirs for that day. The only other time you got aboard was when you got sick and they had to take you to the nurse or the "sick cabin" for a few days of rest or something, a ride that none of us wanted to take

———

After lights out one night later in the week, I heard John, our cabin counselor, say, "Don't wake him up."

I opened my eyes to see John and three other older campers picking up Gene Ostrowski on the sheet from his bed and carry him to the cabin door. It was really dark outside, but there was just enough light to see that they were moving down toward the lake with him.

"One, two, three!" echoed from the pier that jutted out into the lake followed by a loud splash then the scream that bounced off the trees, walls, and sky. "Help, I'm drowning! Help me!"

I heard the running of heavy feet as the older campers passed my cabin and disappeared into the maze of the other buildings.

The splashing continued for a while but then petered out. A few minutes later Gene sloshed back into our cabin crying softly, teeth chattering and whimpering, all at the same time.

"What's wrong, Gene?" I asked sleepily.

"I just got tossed in the lake."

"Who did it, what happened?" I lied.

His teeth chattered, "I don't know; I woke up in the water. Why did they throw me in?"

"Gee, I don't know. Have you done anything wrong lately?" I asked knowing full well that he had "gotten lost" during the Flasher game that night, causing our cabin to be disqualified.

"Do you think it was because of Flasher?" he whined.

"What do you think?"

"Who threw me in?"

I again lied, "Search me."

He suddenly wailed, "I don't like it here."

"Quiet down, you'll wake everybody up, then everyone will really be mad at you," I hissed.

He dropped all his sopping-wet bedding and pajamas on the floor and climbed into his bunk, put his head under the pillow, and started crying. I rolled over and tried to sleep.

Flasher wasn't that bad, once you got the hang of it. He should have stayed with us; walking off into the woods alone was not a good idea. No wonder the counselors were mad. If he had gotten hurt, it would have been a big problem for everyone.

I remember Mr. Levi explaining the rules for Flasher and Whistler the first night in front of the campfire. He said, "Never leave your buddies. Stay together, hold on to the belt of the kid in front of you." He finished his talk with, "If you get lost or can't keep up with your group, sit down, someone will find you. Don't try to find your way back to camp." We were all pretty scared after his talk.

Flasher and whistler were two games that were required for all campers. The game involved having a group of camp staff go into the woods at dusk, taking up positions with either flashlights or whistles, and then either blink or blow to signal their locations. Cabin teams would then run into the woods without flashlights to try finding all of the staff. The first cabin to find all of the flashers or whistlers would win. All campers had to be counted at each location by the staff person in order to make sure that all were there. Learning to stay together in the dark was pretty important. I guess that Gene forgot what Levi had told us. I thought about Gene getting thrown into the lake and said to myself, "I'll bet he doesn't forget again."

Everyone wanted to learn how to shoot a gun. Since there was only one period a day for electives, BB gun was always filled, but cabins with high scores in team sports or activities were given first choice each day. With Gene in our cabin, I did not even get close to BB gun, but put it on my list for the next year.

Making lanyards from thin, colored plastic strips was the craft that most of the campers from lower ranked cabins got to make. I never did get the hang of tying the knots properly and took extra swimming lessons and canoeing. Lucky for me that those classes were not so full since the water was a bit cold in the morning when the lessons started.

Wild sarsaparilla, raspberries, blueberries, and blackberries all grew wild in the sandy soil around camp. Learning how to find, pick and eat the berries, and dig out the sarsaparilla was the best. I had never seen or tasted berries before and thought I had gone to heaven. Finding out that root beer could be sucked out of a root was also neat. Showing the other kids in my cabin how to do it was fun. "Suck on this; it tastes just like root beer!" I told them.

Mumblety-peg was probably the most special skill I learned at camp. Carrying a pocketknife was OK, but doing stuff with it could make you a bigger star than the guy that did Duncan Yo-Yo tricks in the school-yard. We played mumblety-peg every day in front of our cabin. After a few days, I became the person to beat. My specialty was a double flip from my nose to upright in the ground. By the end of the session, I was good with a knife. I never did as well with the Yo-Yo.

I don't remember leaving camp that summer or going home any of the other summers that I spent there. Getting there was great, so was thinking about going again next year. The only thing that I really remember was praying, "Please God, put Gene in a different cabin next year!" After seeing how God was able to take care of all the wild animals at camp, I was pretty sure that getting Gene assigned to another cabin next year would be easy for him. At the least, I prayed that Gene might go on a snipe hunt and never come back.

The Kid Who Got Shot

Our neighborhood was filled with lots of kids, but we never saw them except in the summer when we were all out from school. During the rest of the year, it was either too cold to play outside much, we were studying, at the Y, or at home doing chores. You mostly played with kids from your block or the ones just across the street but not much beyond that. Farther away they were strangers, and we just didn't make friends with them. Sometimes you would play with kids from your school even if they didn't live close to you, but it was not a usual happening. The summer of 1951 was one of those times.

Richard Mulvaney lived over on Milwaukee Avenue, about a block away from the Union Hall. He was two years ahead of most of us in the neighborhood at St. Boniface School, so we didn't see him around very much. In fact, we knew nothing about him, except that he lived on the second floor in a flat behind a store that sold cardboard boxes. He was skinny and stayed by himself most of the time. My mother told me that it was because he had scarlet fever while he was little and had something called a rheumatic heart.

It came as a big surprise to everyone when word spread around the neighborhood that he had been shot and was in the hospital. Since all of us had just seen *Sands of Iwo Jima* and all sorts of war movies and Westerns, we knew that getting shot was a big deal. It was something you die from if you got hit in the right place.

We played at getting shot and shooting people all the time, but this was the first time that anyone real we knew had been shot. My uncle would show us his bullet wounds when he got drunk enough, but to have a real kid actually shot was like having a movie star living next door. Richard went from being a nobody to instant star, just by getting

39

shot. We got shot all the time playing and nobody really cared but I guess that in real life, these things were more serious.

"Where is he?" I asked my mom.

"Over at St. Elizabeth's," she answered.

"Can we go see him?"

"The *Times* says that the police are still questioning him about what happened. Maybe after they're finished you can go."

"When will that be?"

"Don't ask so many questions; I'll see what I can find out and let you know."

That kind of answer usually meant that I'd never get anything more from her about whatever it was that I had asked about. I started asking around the block to see if anyone had heard anything about him.

"I heard he died," said my cousin Bonnie.

"No he didn't," said my other cousin Kenny.

"I heard he just got home from the hospital," said Tommy.

Everyone else had already moved on to other concerns such as, "When are my parents going to take me to Riverview?" "Will the Cubs win any more games before Labor Day." "Will they have anymore grape lindys at the grocery store this week?" Going to ride a rollercoaster or going to a Cubs game and having a flavored ice were just more important than wondering about how it really feels to get shot.

For some reason, Richard's bullet wound was still of concern to me even though I had absolutely nothing to do with him before he got shot. I guess it was like wondering about the hushed voices that were used to describe the "dirty things" that everyone says happened at the beginning of the summer to Carol Ukala. My mother said she was rolled in a rug with some guy from the eighth grade at Holy Trinity. It sounded like a pretty dumb thing to do, but I guess it was pretty bad, as the Sisters at St. Boniface wanted to expel her during the summer before we even began eighth grade. They said she was a bad influence and had "developed too fast." Richard, however, didn't do anything wrong. The best we could understand was that he was just standing there and the next moment, wham, down he went.

The Mulvaney's had two sons, Richard and Robert. Neither of the boys had lots of friends because they didn't play outside very much, so

Richard getting shot was a big change for them. They instantly became friends with everyone. At least everyone wanted to talk with Richard, look at the hole in his body, and generally try to find out what it was like to really be shot.

Robert really didn't know too much about what had happened, as he was with his mother in Gary visiting his grandmother when Richard was shot. Richard and his dad were at home just sitting on the back porch when the bullet came out of nowhere and struck him.

His dad said that he dropped the Miller High Life he was drinking and dove onto the floor of the back porch when the bullet whined past him and struck Richard. He made no sound as the bullet hit him; he just fell over and started bleeding. Mr. Mulvaney had been in the Marines and I guess was used to seeing guys get shot, so he knew what to do. He said he pressed an old dishrag over the spot where he was bleeding and carried Richard over to the Union Hall and used the phone to call the fire department for an ambulance.

The official name of the Union Hall was the Polish Roman Catholic Union. It was on the corner of Milwaukee Avenue and Augusta Boulevard and took up most of the block. The Union had a telephone and some people there helped Mr. Mulvaney until the fire department and police came to move Richard to the hospital.

The Union was like the Y for lots of people in the neighborhood, but my dad said, not as good. I went to one of their summer camps once. I thought it was terrible so after that, I only went to the one that the Division Street Y ran during the summer. It was great; the food was super, especially the onion gravy they used on the mashed potatoes. It didn't have snakes in the water like the muddy swimming hole that the Union used. The Mulvaney's used it because it was on their block and cheaper than the Y.

Richard was shot on a Sunday evening and stayed in the hospital until the following Thursday. My friends who lived closer to the Mulvaney's said that his mom brought him home from the hospital in a taxi. He must have been in real bad shape to come home in a taxi, since they were only used for weddings, funerals, and when going to the train station.

The kids said he walked up the stairs to their flat with just a little help from his mom. They couldn't see any bandages, so we still didn't know where he had been shot.

41

The *Sun Times* had a small story about the shooting on the day he was released from the hospital.

> *Richard Mulvaney, aged 10, was released from St. Elizabeth's hospital today. He was wounded on Sunday of this week by a single shot fired from a 22.cal.-hunting rifle. The shot appeared to have originated from the vicinity of Milwaukee Avenue. The police continue to investigate but to date, they cannot find any reason why the shooting took place. Mulvaney is expected to make a full recovery.*

The newspaper never said where he was shot. Had his guts been spilling out the way they did in the movies? Was there blood all over the floor on the porch that still showed a big dark stain? Did he lose his stomach or a lung? We talked about all of those things happening to him but didn't know if a .22 hunting rifle could do any of them? We really didn't know, but when he got home, we figured we should be able to talk to him and find out.

Mrs. Mulvaney wanted Richard home from the hospital because it was going to be Robert's birthday on Friday. When she knew that Richard would be coming home, she began inviting kids to a birthday party for Robert. I did not get invited at first since Robert was a few years behind me at school, but most of his friends were away on vacation at Lake Geneva, Indiana Dunes, or some other great place and could not come. She could only find two kids to come, and that would not be much of a party.

My cousin Kenny and I went over the see Richard on Friday afternoon hoping that we would be able to see the wound. Mrs. Mulvaney was so glad to see some extra kids that she invited us to the birthday party along with visiting with Richard.

"Wow," Kenny said. "We get to see where he was shot and get some cake too!" Neither turned out to be very great.

At the birthday party, they had some cupcakes with white icing and glasses of cold water with Hershey's chocolate syrup mixed into it. Hershey's syrup and cold water don't mix very well; you just get globs of chocolate floating in the water. Most of them stick to the glass, so you get mostly water to drink and a very yucky-looking glass.

Richard's wound was also disappointing. He had a bandage around his right leg above his knee. We asked him to show us the bullet hole while his mother was cleaning up the party mess.

"OK," he said and pulled up his pajama leg to show it to us. All we saw was a small bandage that he peeled away to show us a red line about the size of a dime with a few black threads holding it together.

"That's it?" I blurted out.

"Yeah," Richard answered. "Not very much to see. It really didn't even hurt that bad when I got shot. Kind of like a hornet sting. The cops made a big deal out of it but after I got to the hospital and they gave me a poke with a needle, I didn't feel a thing, and still don't."

Kenny and I went home, leaving Richard with his leg up on a kitchen chair sitting in about the same place he was when the bullet came from nowhere and made him famous for a few days.

"Funny isn't it?" I said to Kenny. "Richard got famous for being shot, but it really wasn't anything special."

"He's still the same old Richard," Kenny answered. "He didn't even know that he was famous and now that everyone knows it was just a small hole, he's going to be famous but for being more of a jerk than he was before."

"Yeah, and he didn't even have anything to do with either thing happening."

When I got back home, my mom told me that the name Richard, like mine, meant powerful leader. *After looking at him today, I'm sure that's something that he is never going to be, especially in this neighborhood.*

The Hot Dog Stand

T he corner of Noble and Milwaukee Avenue in Chicago was where I found heaven, not in Holy Trinity Church, but next door to it at the Vienna Hot Dog stand. I never knew that food tasted so good. It was so different from what I ate at home. Don't get me wrong, our food at home was OK, but this stuff was great. It was much better than those new TV dinners that had just come out.

I stopped one day to watch from outside the steamed-up window as they made those delicious smelling dogs. The old guy running the place would take a bun, put some poppy seeds on it, steam it to get it soft, then add a hot dog, yellow mustard, bright green relish, sliced tomato, a slice of pickle, chopped onions, and sprinkle on some celery salt. He took a big scoop of french fries and rolled it all together in a sheet of waxed paper and sold it to us for twenty-five cents. If you wanted hot peppers, those were free, but I didn't like them very much, even though you could have all you could eat of them. A Coke was a nickel.

The smell of hot dogs was almost enough to make my mouth water from half a block away. I walked by drooling when going to and from St. Boniface School. It was not a problem when I went to Holy Trinity because that was in the other direction. On the way home after school about three o'clock and hungry was another story. The pull of the yeasty smell from the steamed buns was maddening. The yellow-and-red Vienna Red Hot sign was like a magnet that I resisted for as long as I could.

"Whadda ya gonna have, kid?" the hot dog guy said, peering over the steam table at me.

"One Vienna hot dog, please," I said.

"Everything on it?"

"Yes," I nodded my head.

"Anything else?"

"Coke."

"Gotcha. Let's see two bits for the dog, nickel for the suds. Gimme thirty cents."

I carefully counted out the pennies, nickels, and dime that I had saved from my movie money and said, "Here it is."

"OK kid, enjoy," he said. Then he added, "You're new, right?"

I nodded.

"You know about shooting the bear?"

I shook my head.

"Well, that dog you have there could be free if you hit the bear's stomach ten times in a row."

Wow, I thought, *free hot dogs. All I have to do is shoot the bear in the stomach ten times in a row. What bear, shoot it with what, when, how often could I do this and get free hot dogs?* All these questions washed over me while I was standing below the tall counter and reaching up to get at my first hot dog.

"Oh, OK, thanks," I said.

"You look like a good shot. Here, try the first game on me," he said, pointing at a strange-looking contraption along the back wall of the stand. He handed me a token. "Eat up first; don't let the dog get cold. Then try it."

I nodded again and began to open the greasy paper and look for the ketchup bottle. *A hot dog and a free game: What could possibly be better? Getting free dogs for shooting the bear,* I thought. *I'm not ten until August and already I'm getting free stuff!*

I watched the bear as it walked back and forth across the clearing in the forest. It was about a foot tall, covered in black fur with glass windows on both of its sides and on its belly. It was inside a glass-covered cage. A rifle was attached to the contraption by a rubber hose about eight feet long. The object of the game was to use the light beam that came out of the barrel of the rifle when you pulled the trigger to hit the small circular glass windows on the side of the bear. If you hit it, the bear would rise up and turn his stomach toward you. You then had to hit the round glass window on his stomach ten times before the game ended. You had two minutes to play each round.

45

I was about halfway done with my dog as I watched an old delivery guy take a few turns at the bear. He would try hitting the bear and then keep shooting at his stomach until he ran out of time. He got six hits on it and then said something like, "Shit." He slammed the gun down and stormed out of the place. The counter guy laughed and said, "Don't worry about it, kid; he never gets more than six. He's a lousy shot! Four years in the Army and he still can't shoot worth a good Goddamn!"

I swallowed hard and nodded to him.

It seemed like it took me half an hour to finish my dog and get up the nerve to try the gun. I put in the token and managed to hit the bear three times and got the stomach once before time ran out. I put the gun down and studied the game for a few minutes before picking up my books and heading for the door.

"See you again, kid. Keep practicing," he said as I pushed my way back onto Noble Street for the walk home. *How am I going to get the money to practice shooting the bear? It's gonna cost ten cents per game, so if I could "get the bear," my hot dog would only cost me a dime instead of quarter. Where would the money come from? I need to find some money.*

Much to my surprise, the answer was right in front of me when I got home that afternoon. My sister, Dee, was five years older than me and in high school. She was home early from class and working on her coin collection when I got there. She had lots of those blue fold-up books that you used to put coins in from different years and locations until you filled up the books. She once said my mother got her started ten years ago and her books were getting full with coins from the 1920s, '30s, and '40s.

It took me about five minutes to figure out that if I borrowed some of the older coins from the back of those books, she would not remember that they were there. I would then be able to "kill the bear" with some practice and then save money on all the hot dogs I ever wanted to eat. I could use the savings to put the coins I borrowed back in her books before she knew they were gone.

Getting the coins was easy after that since Dee was at school late and didn't often have time to look after her blue books. I kept borrowing coins, practicing after school, and got my score up to steady sevens and eights after about two weeks. I got a nine once but my hot dogs were few and far between, as I was spending more money on the bear than on food. I had also cleaned out the '20s and '30s from her books, and I was getting worried that she might notice the big gaps where coins had clearly been in the cutouts on the pages.

I also remembered that I had a black Cash Register bank that my parents were filling for me to go to summer camp. I found a way to open the rear of the bank without it showing. I began taking money from it to keep killing the bear, and getting an occasional hot dog, or maybe a Mexican tamale. They were only ten cents but nowhere as good as a dog. Some of the older kids said they were made with rat meat. I didn't know what rat meat tasted like, but they were pretty good.

I got my first "ten" exactly seven weeks after I ate my first dog. We had only a week left of school and then off to the YMCA summer camp, where I would be shooting a real BB gun. When I got back from practicing at camp, I should be eating free hot dogs all the time.

I didn't have enough money to stop at the hot dog stand the next day, so I came right home to try getting some more money from my bank. I walked right into the worst problem ever. I got "found out" by my sister. She started with, "Have you been in my stuff?" the minute I walked in the door. She had the blue books in her hand.

"Why would I touch your coins?" I began.

"Who said anything about coins?"

"I don't know," I stammered.

"Wait till your mother gets home; you're really gonna get it!" she yelled and stormed back into her room and pulled the curtain shut.

"I didn't do nothing!" I shouted after her.

My mother arrived home about six and my dad about an hour later. Since it was staying light out late already, she told me to go outside and play until they called me. It took about half an hour before my dad called me into the house. He had his razor strap in his hand. Before we even talked about what I did, he whacked me several times across my butt and legs with the strap. That really got my attention. I screamed like a little girl.

He then asked, "Why were you stealing money from your sister's coin collection and from your camp money?"

"I wasn't stealing; I borrowed it…I'm gonna repay it from my meal savings," poured out of my mouth between the tears.

For that answer I got several more whacks across my back and butt.

"You're not going to camp this year either!" he yelled. "It's stealing; don't tell me it's not. What the hell's wrong with you?"

"I wasn't stealing," I wailed. "I was going to return it; that's not stealing."

For that answer I got several more whacks before he said, "Goddamn it, it's stealing. She didn't give it to you, did she? You just took it when nobody was around. That's stealing, no matter what you said you were going to do about returning it later."

"Near as your mother and I can figure out, you took about fifteen dollars from your sister's coin collection. We don't know what that's really worth if she had sold the coins to a dealer. You also took another six dollars and fifty cents from your own bank. Are you that dumb that you steal from yourself?" he asked.

"I was going to put it all back, honest!" I sobbed.

"Yes, you're going to pay it all back. Where did you spend it?"

"Hot dog stand," I mumbled.

"Hot dog stand?" he repeated. "Where? Which one?"

"On the corner."

"Vienna Red Hot?"

I nodded.

"First off, you are never to set foot inside that stand again. Second, you come home right after school and stay here. Since you like different food that you can't get here, you can just start cooking all our meals with the great stuff you like."

"I don't know how to cook," I whispered between sobs.

"Well you better learn. After hanging out at that hot dog stand, you should be an expert in fancy foods."

"But," I began, but he raised his hand that was still holding the strap. I stopped.

"Starting tomorrow, you will make dinner every night. If you make nothing, we eat nothing. Start using that fancy food education you paid for with stolen money."

He stopped, turned my head to face him, and continued, "If I ever hear that you took anything else from anybody, I'll cut off your hand.

That's what they did to thieves in my village. Polish people don't put up with thieves. Don't ever do it again; however you call it, it's stealing."

I swallowed hard and nodded my head that I understood.

———

"What's that?" my sister asked the following evening when she got home from school.

"Dinner."

"I hope your father beats you again," she said. "That looks terrible." She always said "your father" when she was mad about something to remind me that he wasn't "her father."

"Too bad. That's dinner tonight."

"Wait until they get home; I'm looking forward to seeing you get beaten again."

When my mom and dad got home, we sat down to eat. I brought my first dinner to the table. It was boiled hot dogs, noodles with ketchup, and canned peas. The noodles were not hot and the hot dogs looked limp compared to what I had been eating, but I made it. My parents ate it without saying anything and left me to clean up the dishes and the mess I made getting dinner ready. My sister just scowled.

When my dad got up from the table, he opened the cabinet over the stove and pulled out his bottle of Jim Beam whiskey. He poured himself a shot, drank it, and went toward the living room. He turned, "So, what are you making for dinner tomorrow?"

Cardboard Boxes

We first saw them next to the railroad tracks on Friday afternoon. There were piles and piles of the biggest boxes that any of us had ever seen. It looked like one of the railroad boxcars had opened its doors and someone dumped everything in it off onto the embankment and into the dirt lot that faced my grandmother's house on Troop Street. The pile was about halfway up the large light colored stone blocks that went up almost two stories. The bums, that sometimes lived in the wall, were not around. Nobody worked at the factory on weekends. Those boxes were there for the taking.

"Boy, these are heavy," Bonnie said, as she struggled to drag a box across the street to our gangway. Ellen, from over on the next block, helped her.

"She's strong," Ellen added brightly. Bonnie blushed.

"What are you going to do with them?" I asked.

"Play house."

"Gosh, they're enough there to play city."

"Very funny, want to play with us?"

"Who else is coming over?"

"Carol, Danuta, and Ellen."

"Can I ask Kasz and Gene?"

"Kasz, but not Gene."

"Why not Gene?"

"He's icky. I don't like him."

"Gene's icky? Why?"

"He's always dirty and I don't know...I just don't want him playing in my boxes."

"Your boxes? I thought they were anyone's boxes who dragged them home?"

She harrumphed and continued dragging the box across the street.

"If you want him to play, build your own house or city or whatever you want to do, but leave us alone."

That was easy to decide. We had lots of room around both houses on our lot so I dragged my first box over to my grandmother's house on the corner. Bonnie dropped hers outside the house next door to where we both lived. I went to get Kasz and Gene.

By the time it was dark we had mounds of boxes piled up next to the iron railings that kept people from falling into the walkway that was about four feet below street level and wound it's way around the house. It looked like we hadn't even touched the pile of boxes next to the tracks.

"How many of those things did they dump there?" Kasz asked.

"Don't know but I can't carry any more tonight. My mom is going to be calling me for dinner soon. Let's start again early tomorrow."

He turned and walked south on Troop Street toward his house. "OK, see you."

"Co robisz?" My grandmother shouted as I started walking into the gangway.

"Neitz," I answered.

"Nie rozumiem," she yelled.

"I'm building a house," I said, this time louder.

My Aunt Mary came out and talked to her about what Bonnie and her friends were doing and she calmed down.

"You need to have all this stuff cleaned up by the time the rag picker's wagon comes on Monday so she can sell the stuff that you dragged home."

"She wants to sell our boxes to the rag man?"

"After you're done with them."

"Tak," said Granma, her head bobbing up and down.

"Tak," said Mary.

They both looked at me and waited for my answer.

"Tak," I said, without much pleasure. Kasz and Gene were not going to be happy. I decided not to tell them until later in the weekend.

Granma gave me a toothless smile, nodded, and muttered, "Dziękuję," and turned back into the entryway for her building.

Aunt Mary and I nodded to her.

Aunt Mary said, "Just play with that stuff until you get tired of it. Let's see what you say then."

I shook my head and walked upstairs for dinner.

The weather was just turning warm. All the snow had melted in the shady parts of the gangway and the sky was bright blue when we started building our playhouses.

Kasz and I made a few more trips across the street and got a few more boxes just before some of the rag pickers pulled up with their wagons and started loading stuff up.

"Watch out, don't drag that box through the horse poop," I yelled to Kasz.

"Darn horses, they would have to show up before we finished getting our stuff," he said.

By the time we got the last of our building boxes, there were four wagons there being loaded. The loads were so big they were tipping the wagons to the side.

"Think the horse can move that load?" I asked

"I don't know. Where do they go with this stuff?"

"Beats me."

Just then one of the wooden wagons began turning around with a load of boxes swaying off the back. The horse turned too sharply and the wagon tipped slightly, then more and more.

"Look, it's in slow motion," I shouted.

"Wow!" the other kids shouted as the wagon slowly turned on its side with the boxes still tightly tied to its wooden frame. The old man driving was dumped out still holding his long whip. He landed on the pile of boxes that were still on the ground. His round black hat went flying.

"Holy smokes, just like the movies," Gene shouted.

"You OK, mister?" I said, running over to where the old man was lying in a heap, his dirty overcoat spread open like a big dead moth.

"OK," he muttered, looking around. "Help," he said, pointing to the wagon and moving his hands up and down.

He said something that I didn't understand but Gene did.

"He wants us to help him get the wagon back up," Gene said.

"Tell him sure, what can we do?"

Gene told us, and we got a bunch of kids playing stickball down the block. We all helped unload the boxes and pushed the wagon upright with help from a few of the older men standing around watching. When he got the horse hitched, he backed the wagon up to the pile, loaded it up again, and clopped off down Troop Street toward Milwaukee Avenue. He waved to us as he snapped his whip and raised his hat to the men that helped him.

A car sped up behind the wagon, swerved, and then quickly passed him so close that he had to stop until it got by. He yelled something at them I didn't understand and shook his fist.

Two other wagons had come and gone while he was reloading and the pile was almost gone. We were lucky to have what now looked like two or three wagonloads of boxes; it was good we got there early.

"What's that by your house?" Gene asked.

"I don't know," I said, looking at the series of upright boxes stacked together into the passageway next to our house. "Looks like Captain Gallant's fort in the desert."

"Yeah, right out of the *Foreign Legion* movies," said Kasz.

"Who built it?" I said.

"We did," said Bonnie and Danuta, sticking their heads out of a window they cut into the closest box.

"Ah, we can do better than that," said Gene grabbing a box and throwing it onto our pile.

"Yeah, well let's see you do it then," the girls giggled, sticking their tongues out.

"OK, let's show 'em," Kasz said.

And we started.

By dinnertime our fort stretched in three directions along the walkway between the raised sidewalk and my grandmother's house. It also went up about one and a half stories. I borrowed a knife from my Uncle Stanley's apartment and cut out windows and doors. Gene and Kasz were helping when my mom called me for dinner. "Gotta go. See you later," I told them.

Kasz and Gene worked for a while more until they heard their moms yelling for them to get home.

After dinner I started watching Jackie Gleason on the television and forgot about the fort.

The next morning I remembered I was supposed to put the knife back and clean up the scraps of what we had cut away from the boxes we were using for the walls, floors, and ceilings of our fort. I rushed out to get started even before breakfast since we were going to nine o'clock mass. I wanted to have everything the way it was supposed to be before my parents and grandmother came out to see what we had built.

The knife was gone. I looked all over the fort, under the boxes we had not yet used, in the scrap pile, everywhere.

Nothing.

I was still pulling things apart looking for it when Uncle Stanley pushed his head in through a window and growled at me. "Com-ere!" He looked terrible and smelt worse—probably from being out all night drinking.

"Jud' u take my knife?" he slurred.

I nodded.

"So wher'se it?"

"It was right here," I said, pointing to the floor of the box.

"Wher'se it now?"

"I don't know, I think somebody took it."

"Yeah, I took it," he growled again.

"You took it?"

"If u wanna use my stuff, you bet'er take care of it," he said, handing me back the knife.

"Thank you. It won't happen again," but he was already gone and walking back to the basement. One of the boxes near the back of the fort was wet and smelled like someone had taken a pee on it. There was also an old jacket balled up like a pillow in the next compartment. It looked like he might have fallen asleep there the night before and was just coming back from using the toilet under the sidewalk when I got into the box. No wonder he found the knife.

I cut some extra cardboard and put it over the wet spot on the floor and cut another window over it to let some of the smell out before I had to get dressed for church.

———

"Hey, it smells in here," Gene said.

"Smells like a cat peed in here," Kasz added.

"I guess so," I said, "but let's not worry about it and get finished building this thing."

We added more and more boxes, cutting more windows, more passages, hidden rooms, and trapdoors. It was amazing. It covered every inch on the passageways, most of the gangways, and went up almost two stories. It started to tip over when Kasz climbed into the upper level, so we made that off limits except in an emergency.

"Hey girls," we yelled, "come see our fort."

"No, thank you," they said.

"Why not? It's pretty great," we shouted to them across the gangway.

"No," they again said.

"Well, then can we see your house?"

"Sure, come in," Bonnie answered.

Their house covered one section of the gangway but was completely furnished inside. Some of the walls were even painted with tempera colors or crayons and they had used rags to make curtains for the cutout windows. They were having a tea party when we crawled through their front door.

"Wow, this is really cool," we said.

"We like it," Danuta answered with a smirk on her bright, rosy cheeks.

"How about coming over to look at our fort?" I asked.

"It smells bad over there," Ellen said.

"No, it doesn't, we aired it out, a cat got into it last night," I said.

"It wasn't a cat," they said laughing.

"Yes, it was," I said.

"I saw Stanley sleeping there early this morning when I went to look inside your fort," said Bonnie. "He was laying around the corner snoring and it smelled like he peed on himself again. I think I woke him up when I was leaving."

"Oh."

"I'm not going over there again, but if you girls want to go, it's up to you," she said.

"Honest, it doesn't smell, we made some windows and covered up the wet spots with lots of cardboard," I told them.

We led Danuta and Ellen on a tour of the fort, including the upper floors, but Gene had to lean against the boxes from the sidewalk while they were crawling around up there.

"Amazing!" they said when they got back outside. "That is some maze in there. How did you guys think that up?"

Kasz and I grinned at each other, shrugged our shoulders. "Don't know; it just kind of happened."

I tried to return the knife to Uncle Stanley, but he didn't answer the door. I pounded for another minute then opened the door, put the knife on his kitchen table, and went upstairs for dinner. Kasz and Gene also were gone with promises to return after school to continue working on our fort so we could play foreign legion.

I rushed home by three fifteen expecting to find Gene and Kasz ready to stand off hundreds of charging Bedouin fighters. Instead I found the last of the boxes being loaded on the wagon of the rag picker with my grandmother talking with him as he worked.

"Where's my fort?" I yelled. "Where did it go?"

My grandmother turned to me and said, "Jesteś głupi."

"That's my stuff on the wagon," I yelled again. She shrugged.

"Cicho!" she snapped.

She turned back to the peddler who gave her some money, gave me a sad smile, climbed up on his wooden wagon seat, snapped the reigns, and started moving slowing toward Troop Street. He turned right and disappeared from view, taking our dreams for protecting the city with him.

Just then Gene and Kasz came around the corner yelling, "Did you see the rag picker just now? He has lots more boxes!"

They stopped as they noticed that our fort and Bonnie's dollhouse were both gone.

"What happened? Where's our stuff?" they shouted.

"Ask her," I said pointing to my grandmother.

She smiled at all of us, put the money into her tiny purse, and slowly walked to the stairway down into the courtyard. Step by step she moved away from where we had the best fort in the world.

How were we going to keep those vicious desert fighters from taking over the city without our fort? To her, the cardboard was only some money; to us, it was the last defense in the desert against the heathen hordes from the East.

56

Aunt Josie

Amotorcycle hit my grandmother on Division Street. It broke her left leg in two places, and she spent two weeks in County Hospital. We had to take care of blind Aunt Josie while she was there.

Aunt Josie lived in the back bedroom in my grandmother's second story apartment across the gangway from my house. If she opened her living room window, she could talk to us on our porch without going outside. We could also hear everything that went on over there—all the time!

Aunt Josie listened to Polish church music all day long. Mass started while it was still dark in the mornings. The music and sermons were on until late in the evening.

"Is she one of the mystics that Sister Jude is always talking about?" asked Kasz while we were sitting on my porch one spring afternoon after school.

"Boy, I don't know, but she sure seems to have only one station on her radio," I said.

"Do they have Polish mystics?" he asked.

"Don't know, but they tell me that Poles are supposed to have the smartest scientists and best musicians, doctors, and soldiers. They even saved General Washington when he was fighting the Redcoats."

"Yeah, but my parents say that our relatives came across Europe and beat everyone, including the Poles, so they can't be too great."

"Really, they beat the Poles?"

"Genghis Khan and his hordes rode across all of East Europe and killed almost everyone, took the rest as slaves, and then went back home."

"Wow, I didn't know that. You related to any of them?"

"Lots of us from the Ukraine have Tartar blood."

Just then my Aunt Mary called out for some help and waved for me to come up to her apartment. I left Kasz and ran upstairs to find Aunt Josie on the floor. She had fallen asleep in her chair and tumbled off and could not get up.

I yelled for Kasz. "Quick, come up here and give me a hand!" I could not look directly at Josie, as her eyes were not there; it was just dark where they should have been. It was scary to see somebody who looked through you instead of at you. Lying on the floor with the sunlight streaming in on her face was even worse. I could see that her eyelids were wet with what looked like tears and her eyeballs were dancing around behind them. I thought they were trying to get out, but she was squeezing them tight to keep them in. I had to turn away.

With my Aunt Mary pulling and Kasz and I pushing, we were able to get her big, soft body back onto her chair. She had on an old housecoat, worn cloth slippers, and a big dark gray knit sweater. It smelled like wet dog close to her. Aunt Mary waved us out of the apartment without another word and turned back with a damp rag toward Josie.

Nobody ever talked about whose aunt Josie was. For all I knew she could have been a stranger that my grandmother was taking care of because she didn't have any other place to go. I asked Aunt Mary and she said to ask my mother; my mother said to ask Buscia. I didn't dare ask her.

There were lots of aunts and uncles that lived with friends and neighbors in the neighborhood. Some were DPs, some were relatives that came from the old country to settle, and others were not well and were sent to stay in America where they could get a good doctor. Families were taking care of each other until they got better, moved, or died.

Aunt Josie died one night. My mother said she had something wrong with her sugar and she died from it. I told my mom to make sure she bought a different kind of sugar so we didn't get sick from what kind it was that Josie used. She laughed.

We all had to go to Polish Mass for Josie's funeral. It lasted a long time in church and the ride to St. Adalbert's Cemetery was even longer, but the food was good at the lunch.

If one of the aunts or uncles got sick, someone would take them to the Apteka on Noble Street to get some medicine, herbs, or roots to boil for tea. If that didn't work, a trip to a real doctor was next. Going to County was something that nobody wanted to do.

"They take you there to die," Aunt Mary said when I asked her about Josie dying at home.

"Well she died here," I said. "What's the difference?"

"Big difference," she said. "Nobody in our family goes to the welfare. Poor people go there when they have nobody to take care of them. She had someone to take care of her."

"But she died anyway."

"It was her time; everybody dies. It was just her being called by God."

"But if she saw a doctor and he fixed her, would that make God angry if she didn't come when he called her the first time?" I asked. "You get mad if I don't come when you call me."

"That's not the same thing. When it's your time, your body knows, whether you have a good doctor, no doctor, or the County. You just go. Ask your Uncle Stanley about it, he knows."

Most of the people on our block were Polish. The next few blocks were mixed Polish, with some Russians, Ukrainians, Lithuanians, and some Czechoslovakians, but still most of us were Polish. You could see who was not Polish when the welfare truck came around with war surplus food that they gave out every once in a while.

The city truck would drive into the neighborhood and park in the middle of our block halfway between our house and the Dew Drop. They would open the back and start stacking the dark green war surplus cans of powdered eggs, flour, sugar, lard, and sacks of potatoes on the tailgate.

Word spread without anyone saying the truck was there. Old ladies would walk to the truck and take a bag of flour, eggs, or whatever they wanted. The lines would form up and move along until everything was gone. The doors would close and the truck would drive away. I only saw them come into the neighborhood two times.

My mom and I were coming back from the loop and the line had about a dozen women and a few old men standing in it. When we walked by the truck, I saw that they had sacks of sugar they were doling out to people using metal cups and pouring it into brown paper bags.

59

"Is this where Aunt Josie went to get her bad sugar?" I asked my mom.

"What are you talking about?"

"You said she died from bad sugar."

"No, it wasn't this sugar, but never take anything from the County; you earn it or get it from your family. We take care of ourselves, not like these DPs, Ukrainians, and Russians. Do you see any of your friends out here begging from the County?"

"No, I guess not."

"That's right, nobody is out here. You earn your money and buy what you need; don't wait for the County to give it to you. They can just as easily take it away from you."

We walked on.

———

"Hey kid, help me get this stuff down to the basement," my Uncle Stanley said as I reached the gangway to our house.

He was carrying some of the things that Aunt Josie had been using before she died.

"Sure, where do you want me to put them?" I said picking up a bundle of clothing that was wrapped in an old, gray, stained bed sheet. "Is this stuff clean?" I asked him.

"What'ja worried about, it won't kill ya," he laughed half-drunkenly.

"It just looks dirty s'all."

"This ain't shit. If you was stripping bodies after some Jap tore open their belly with a bayonet and their guts was running over their pants, that would be different," he said without looking up from sorting.

"You had to do that?" I said turning slightly green.

"You did what you had to do to survive. Guys were dying all the time: shot, gangrene, malaria, dengue fever, elephantitis, gutted, blown-up. No matter how they got there, it was all still the same place. Dying like she did was easy: in her own bed, clean, quiet, and peaceful. Better'n being beaten to death by a Jap officer with a two-by-four. Lots easier."

He became very quiet and stopped sorting and stared at the floor for a while. All I could hear was his breathing.

He suddenly looked around and saw me standing there.

"Listen kid, you take care of yourself 'cause nobody is going to do it for you. Don't listen to anyone who tells you different. Com'hr." He motioned me to come closer. He pulled up his sleeve, showing me the ragged scar that started at his wrist and ended above where his shirt was pulled over his elbow.

I slowly moved over to where I could see what he was trying to show me.

"See this scar?"

"Um hum."

"The Japs did that."

He had told me about the scar once before when he was really drunk, but I nodded my head like it was the first time I had heard his story.

"They caught me taking the pants from a guy that died and changing them for mine that were worn out. They stunk from dysentery but didn't have holes in them like my old ones." He paused, lost in thought.

"Anyways, the young skinny guard watching us saw me changing pants and thought I was trying to hide some food or something. He told the other guards, and they grabbed me and held me down. The kid must have been barely old enough to be in the army but wanted to show who was in charge. He took his bayonet and stuck it into my left arm just below my shoulder and pulled it down to my wrist."

I winced but said nothing.

"I must have passed out 'cause a few days later, I remember the guys holding me down saying that if they didn't clean out the pus and dead skin, they would have to take off my arm."

He went quiet again.

"I screamed for a long time until they finished sewing up the cut with an old needle and some thread. They poured some sulfa powder on it. Guess it worked, my arm is still here," he said, waving it around.

"Anyway, what I'm trying to tell you is that you can rely on your family, and we were family in that Goddamn jungle, to take care of you. Everybody else, fuck them, 'specially the Army. They got us in that stinking place but couldn't get us out. Lots of my buddies and friends died in bad places, some of their bodies we never could get out or even bury right. Fucking animals and bugs ate them right in front of us, nothing we could do."

Tears ran quietly down his face.

"Josie at least died good. Ma took care of her right. The way it should be done. She couldn't control when she died but took care of how she did it the best she could. Can't ask for more than that from anyone."

He stopped, got up, and walked back into his basement apartment and closed the door. I could hear him sobbing softly.

I tied all of Josie's things into the other sheet that Uncle Stanley had there and put everything in the hallway outside Aunt Mary's apartment. She would be helping my grandma take the bundles to Holy Trinity basement to give to the poor.

From what Uncle Stanley said, God didn't much care how or when you died. Whatever was the right time was the right time. It was not something that anyone had any control over. It just happened. If you were lucky, friends and relatives were there and it was a clean place.

His friends died in the rain and the mud, while screaming in pain or crying for their families. Remembering those it happened to badly seemed worse than actually doing it yourself. Maybe having family there for your last breath in a clean bed was better.

Christmas in the Loop

"I can't see out the window; there's too much ice on it!" I yelled to my sister.

Mid-December in Chicago can be really cold and snowy. The snow had almost filled in the gangway between our houses. My buscia had me out there shoveling snow so she could get out of her building. It was up to my shoulders but real powdery so it was light to move.

The oil stove in our living room made that room nice and warm after being outside, but the rest of the house was freezing. On a day like this, you couldn't see the curtains move because the ice froze the frames shut. It stopped the breeze from coming through the house and made it warmer. I could lay under a pierzyna in front of the TV being warm and look at Christmas catalogues.

It was the year Bob Hope's movie, *The Lemon Drop Kid,* opened and it snowed and snowed and snowed. In the loop you could hear "Silver Bells" playing on State Street, just the way it did in the movie. It was really great walking around the loop even though you couldn't feel your fingers or toes for hours after you got inside the stores to warm up. It was like being in the movie, except it was real.

That Christmas I wanted a 287-piece soldier set. It was not the largest one in the toy catalogue; that had 536 pieces. I thought that it might be the right size for Santa to fit in his pack. I didn't get it. My mom said that Santa did not like war toys. I thought that was strange since his picture was all over the catalogue where they showed his elves making the stuff. I got an erector set instead. My cousin, who lived downstairs, got the soldiers, so we played with them anyway. Uncle Joe thought it was good for kids to play war.

"I'm the Cinnamon Bear with Shoe Button Eyes," were the opening words that announced my favorite radio program every afternoon in the weeks before Christmas. I tried not to miss any episodes. I loved Paddy O'Cinnamon. He and the two kids always had wonderful adventures in their big house. Marshall Field's was the sponsor, and they told you about the great stuff you could get on the fourth floor at their store in the loop.

There was no better place in the entire world than Marshall Field's at Christmas. It had the Cinnamon Bear and everything. The rest of the year it was still the only place I wanted to shop. Kasz and Gene thought I was crazy wanting to go to the loop shopping. "Girls do that," they said. I really didn't care. The store was filled with great stuff from all over the world. Also, my mother worked there, so we got a discount on everything we bought. In the employee store, seconds and returns also sold for less than the marked price. We could get good stuff for the same price as things from Goldblatt's.

The first year Petit Fours, canned pheasant, and plum pudding were sold at Field's my mother bought them all with her employee discount so we could try them for the holidays. They were only OK.

One of the really special things was going to look at the Christmas tree in the Walnut Room on the eighth floor. Sometimes you would have to stand in line for hours and walk past all the people eating and drinking in the restaurant just to see the huge tree in the center of the room. It was almost to the ceiling and full of lights, ornaments, tinsel, strings of berries, and silver garlands. It looked grand with the spotlights shining up on it. There were even piles of gift boxes under it. We wondered what neat stuff might be inside of those big boxes, but they kept the line moving so you could only think about it while you slowly marched past. Even seeing it for two or three minutes was worth waiting in line. You prayed that the line would stop for a few minutes when you were close to the tree. It never happened to me, but my cousins said it did when they were in line. They stood in front of it for five full minutes.

"You were sure lucky," I told them when they got home.

"Yes, we were. Too bad you couldn't see everything the way we did," Bonnie smirked.

"Yeah, I guess so. Maybe next time."

"I doubt it."

Even for Field's employees, eating in the Walnut Room was expensive. If we were downtown for a shopping trip, we would either eat at the big restaurant with the soda fountain on State and Randolph, or the Chinese one near Lake Street. Both of them were good. One time I had something called Egg Fu Young. It tasted different but wonderful, even though I never found the eggs in the thick brown sauce. A root beer float with a hamburger and fries was much better, especially on a snowy day. We didn't eat out very much, but you couldn't take a lunch with you downtown, as there was no place to sit and eat it. It was also too far to go home to eat when you were only halfway through shopping.

"I want to see the windows," I announced to my mother while we finished lunch.

"We need to finish up shopping first. I thought you might want to go to the fourth floor first?"

"Sure, then we can see the windows later?"

"I need to pick up a few things, so I'm going to let you walk around by yourself for a while, all right?"

"OK, great. Where do I meet you?"

She looked at the wall clock over the soda fountain and said, "How 'bout we meet at the model railroad train set-up about two o'clock? You have about an hour."

"Sure, great," I stammered.

Off we went through the crowds to Field's. She went to the basement, and I took the escalator to the fourth floor all alone. There were aisles and aisles of dolls, pull toys, windup toys, Tinker Toys, Erector sets, Lincoln Logs, cooking sets, tea sets, puzzles, and games. Kids were everywhere, running and pulling their parents to show them the toys they wanted Santa to bring. I went to look at the battlefield display with thousands of toy soldiers from every kind of war: WWI, WWII, Civil War Blue and Gray, Roman soldiers, and even some on elephants I couldn't identify.

What a sight! Even if there was no chance that Santa was going to bring any of it to your house, it was wonderful. The detail on the soldier's uniforms was amazing. I could see *CSA* on the Civil War belt buckles of the foot soldiers and *USA* on the flannel covering of WW1 canteens. Even if I wanted to buy a set and not wait for Santa to bring it, the cost of one soldier was more than my mom paid for both our lunches.

65

I wandered over to where the crowds were moving around the big area set up as a railroad display. It must have covered as much space as my house and the one below us, and it was just filled with dozens of train displays. There were villages covered with snow, desert areas filled with Santa Fe trains, along with Indians and teepees. There were big city areas that looked like the loop with Burlington trains and lots and lots of others that I'd never seen before. I kept looking around for my mom to make sure I didn't miss her in the crowd, but she wasn't there yet.

There were several very well-dressed women who were walking around the train display talking to the kids watching the trains. One came up behind me and said, "Hello, young man."

I turned around and looked at a very pretty woman who was smiling at me. She said, "What would you like for Christmas?"

"Well, I've asked Santa for one of the WWII 287-piece war sets, and I sure would love one of these trains," I said, pointing at the setup behind me.

"How about some Lincoln Logs instead?"

"No, thank you. I really don't like them very much."

"Come now," she said. "Aren't they fun to play with?"

"The little kids like them, I don't."

"Even if they were a gift to you?"

"Yes um, I wouldn't play with them."

"You sure?" she finally said.

Just then, Mom walked up.

There were several people who had gathered around the lady and me while we were talking. My mom had a hard time getting next to me.

"I'm sure," I said just as my mom pulled my arm and hissed at me to say "yes" to the lady.

I turned to her and said loudly, "Why is everyone trying to get me to take the logs? I don't like them."

Hearing what I told my mother, the pretty woman and the crowd disappeared, leaving us standing alone in the center of the crowd around the train display.

My mother said, "What's wrong with you? That woman works for Lincoln Logs. It's her job to give away big sets of their toys to deserving kids at Christmas for free. She picked you out to get one."

"How was I supposed to know what she was doing? She asked me if I liked them and I told her I didn't."

"You could have taken it as a gift for someone else. It was free."

"But I don't like that stuff. I'd be lying to her."

My mom seemed angry about something as we walked back through the crowds to the down escalator. By the time we got to the street and pulled on our coats, scarfs, and gloves, she seemed to calm down.

It was starting to get dark and Christmas lights were coming on along State Street. The crowds looked bigger than ever. People were three and four deep at the Field's window displays. It took us a long time to work our way south, stopping at each window and waiting till the crowd thinned so we could get a good look. Each window was better than the last with moving people singing Christmas carols, ice skating mice, toy soldiers marching around, and kids sitting under the tree opening presents. One window looked just like the Cinnamon Bear house.

"Let's walk down and look at Carson's and the other stores," I begged.

"You looked at them last time we were here."

"They may have changed them."

"OK, but just a quick look. Then we can get on the EL down there."

Carson Pirie & Scott's windows were nice but not as special as those at Field's. The good thing was that the crowds were not as big, so we were able to walk past in half the time. Before I knew it, we were walking down the stairs to the train for home. There were no seats, but it seemed like only a few minutes before we got off and walked up to the Division and Ashland station.

"Why did we get off here?" I asked my mom while I looked up at the snow that was falling softly. A layer of it just started to cover the old dirty crust from the snow a few days earlier.

"I need to stop at Walgreens. Besides, the Milwaukee Avenue bus doesn't run so often on Saturday, so we would be waiting a long time at Grand Avenue."

"OK, but it's snowing again."

"It's winter in Chicago, it snows. Don't be a baby."

"My feet are cold. I'm not wearing my galoshes. It was nice when we left."

"Well, walk in my footprints then."

We walked to Walgreens, got her stuff, and headed for home down Division Street. It wasn't a long walk home, but following in footprints was not so much fun. They were small and close together. I didn't like doing it very much because there were piles of snow all over the place that I really wanted to climb over. Walking in a straight line was cold, boring, and took too long to get anywhere.

We walked in front of the church where they had shoveled the sidewalk and down the block turning on our street. "I'll run ahead," I said as we got to Noble Street. Nothing was plowed from the last snow and there were only had a few ruts where cars had gotten through the drifts that covered the streets and sidewalks.

"Be careful," she yelled, but I was already climbing over the first big mound of snow. I turned to watch her walking in the middle of the street trying to follow the traces of the tire tracks that turned onto our street.

My Uncle Joe said that Chicago believed in using the best snow removal system in the world. It was something called spring. Whatever it was, I was in no hurry for it to get here: the piles were too much fun. Besides, it made Santa's job at lot easier.

Christmas Holidays

We got the first flocked tree in the neighborhood. It was white with blue floodlights, and we centered it in the living room picture window. It was the only one on Cortez Street in 1953. My dad and I went to get it from a store, not a tree lot, on December twentieth. My mom was not so happy because we had to move the furniture so the tree could be seen from the street. She probably was happy though because it made our house look special, not quite like Candy Cane Lane on Oak Park Avenue between Belmont and Addison, but better than the other houses on our block.

Nothing looked better before the Christmas holidays than Candy Cane Lane, even if you froze your ears off driving in the slow-moving traffic circling all the streets. All the windows in the car had to be rolled down because you couldn't see the lights and decorations if the windows fogged up and turned to layers of ice.

The day after our tree went in front of the window, Wally and Frank both said it looked really cool. Gene, my Ukrainian friend, asked, "When are you going to take it down?"

"We just put it up, why worry about when we'll take it down?" I said.

"Well, my Christmas is later than yours, and I'll take the tree when you are done using it," he said.

"What? You want our used Christmas tree?"

"Sure, my dad does it all the time, and I'll bet he'll really like this one."

"You don't pay for your trees?"

"Nah, we usually just walk around the neighborhood before New Year's and look to see what's out in the alleys."

"Really?"

"Sure, would you pay for a tree if there were lots of free ones to choose from?"

"I guess not, but don't you worry about getting bugs and stuff from other families?"

"Not really, the baby Jesus protects our house from those things."

"Oh! I never thought about it but I guess it makes sense. He wouldn't want the trees to be wasted. I'll ask my dad if you can have it."

"No, don't do that. Just tell me the night before you're going to take it down and we'll be in the alley to get it."

"Yeah, sure," I said. Wally and Frank didn't say anything.

Christmas was a really big deal in the neighborhood, even for the Russians and Ukrainians. The Jewish kids were always kind of sad because their holiday did not get them lots of toys and gifts like our Christmas.

Gene said, "If the Jewish kids believed in Jesus, maybe he would visit them too, even if their parents didn't go to church."

Wally answered, "Yeah, if they believed in the baby Jesus, at least for the holidays, I'll bet they would find stuff under their tree."

I reminded them that the Jewish families did not have trees. "So how is that going to happen?"

"I don't know," said Wally. He was sure that baby Jesus would find a way.

———

Planning for the holidays started right after Halloween and kept going until all the shopping and sales were done just before New Year's Eve. It made shopping cheaper for Gene and his family since they could buy gifts when all the sales were on.

There were lots of stores in the neighborhood that sold special foods and gifts for traditional celebrations, regardless of where in Eastern Europe your family was from. Ackerman Brothers Fruits & Vegetables, on the corner of Division and Rockwell Streets, was one of them. It had the best stuff in the neighborhood.

"Take this order to Mrs. Rosen on Rockwell," the older Mr. Ackerman told me. "Address is on the box. She's on the third floor in the back."

"OK!" I groaned as I went to get the delivery bike from the back room of the fruit market. I worked there to make some Christmas money. It was hard work, especially when twenty pounds of potatoes, five pounds of onions, several heads of cabbage, and all kinds of fruit needed to be delivered up three flights of snowy stairs.

The delivery boys got fifteen cents per hour and all the tips we collected. Since only one boy worked at a time, you got to carry whatever orders were sold that needed delivery. But getting fifty to sixty pounds up three or four flight of stairs in wooden delivery boxes took some muscles. I usually went home tired and sore. The extra money made up for it, except when the snow was deep and neither bikes nor sleds worked and you had to carry everything all the way to some faraway apartment. Sometimes you got extra-large tips in bad weather. Around Christmas tips were even better.

I really liked the younger Ackerman. He looked just like Jeff Chandler, the movie star. In the winter he wore an old leather jacket with a gray sweatshirt under it that made him look like a body builder. He also let all the workers eat anything from the store they wanted while they were working. "Look," he would say, "eat anything you want: bananas, Bartlett pears, oranges, anything. Just don't take stuff home with you. That's stealing."

He also gave workers discounts for the holidays so our Christmas food shopping was cheaper. His older brother growled at everyone. He yelled and was not nice, even with the customers. I thought he was sick or something since the younger Ackerman was always telling him to "go slow."

In our house, Christmas Eve was always celebrated with baked fish. I never liked it and ate as little as possible. But Christmas day there was usually a goose and all the trimmings. It made up for the fish. Our fish always came from Stop & Shop in the loop. They had more fish than anyone. It was sold from ice-covered counters, in wooden barrels lined up on the sawdust-covered floor. The expensive stuff could be found in glass-front refrigerated counters. I really liked going there.

At home, preparations for Christmas usually started after Thanksgiving when cookie recipes came out and cookie tins were filled with rosettes, almond cookies, gingersnaps, butter cookies, and

Pfeffernusse. The fruitcake had brandy added to it each week. Closets became off limits as they started filling up with gifts. Setting up the tree usually signaled that the final push to finish shopping was getting close. My sister was always yelling, "Stay out of my room," anyway. She just did it more this time of the year.

I could tell that most of the families that used Ackerman deliveries were stocking up for big Christmas and Hanukkah meals. The orders were larger and the tips were better. Holidays looked like they were better for the stores than the customers. Everybody spent more and the stores made more, even delivery boys. After the holidays nobody had money for anything.

Everybody usually worked Christmas Eve until the normal quitting time then rushed home to get dinner ready. We all pitched in and worked at different things to get ready for dinner. I set the table and my sister started dinner until Mom got home and took over. Dad picked up the fish from Stop & Shop.

We usually sat down to eat about seven o'clock. We always set the table for one more person than was expected so that if a stranger knocked on the door there would be a table setting for them to join us for dinner. We never had anyone do it except once. We had just started eating when there was a loud banging on the front door. We all looked at each other. *Was this the time? Was a stranger actually going eat with us?* My dad opened it. It was someone at the wrong house.

When dinner was over, I started clearing plates and found a silver dollar under mine. "Did anyone else have money under their plate?" I asked.

Everyone started lifting their plates. Sure enough, there were silver dollars under each one of them. I had set the table and knew there was nothing under them when we began eating. "A Christmas miracle?" my dad suggested. My sister rolled her eyes. My mom walked into the kitchen. It was never talked about until the following year when it happened again. We all thought it was my dad putting the money there, but we never caught him doing it.

After dinner we opened presents. If we were lucky, we finished before we left for Midnight Mass about eleven thirty. Sometimes, if people came over after church, we would have cookies, coffee, and eggnog, but mostly we just went to bed, tired and happy.

Christmas morning we spent looking at our presents and trying to remember which gift tag went with what package so that thank you notes could be written. Then we tried on all the clothes to figure out what things needed to be exchanged or returned. It was also the day for movies.

The big new movies of the year always had their opening day in the loop on Christmas. I always went to the first show, unless relatives were coming to the house. This was not very often since my mother was always fighting with one sister or the other, so usually nobody came over. This was good because my cousins from the south side were not very nice, especially Joey. He used to beat me up all the time. I tried not to be home if he was coming.

In Chicago, the loop was the heart of the collection of neighborhoods that made up the city. All the subway lines and elevated trains came together to make a loop around the center of downtown. Almost all of the big department stores, big movie theaters, expensive restaurants, and office buildings were there. That's where Christmas was magic. Going there was a big deal, no matter what the occasion, but at Christmas it was a fairyland of lights, people shopping, and decorated store windows. I went there as often as possible, especially for movie openings.

It was only a bus ride and a transfer to the subway to get there. On a holiday it took about forty-five minutes. By going to Midnight Mass we could have breakfast, clean up the mess from the presents, and be in the loop by 9:30 on Christmas morning. We walked around looking at the windows in Marshall Field's and Carson Pirie & Scott and then stood in line for the first show.

Each window along State Street had lots of brightly lighted mechanical scenes of people shopping, stores filled with presents, and nativity stories. If you got there early enough, you could get close to the windows and not have to look between people bundled up in overcoats, scarves, and hats pulled down over their ears. Snow always seemed to come just before Christmas Eve and made shopping and everything else more festive.

Hundreds of people would walk from window to window along State Street looking at all the store displays. It was one of the best parts of the holidays, knowing that everyone from all over the city was doing the same thing and seeing the same stuff. It made everyone into neighbors, even if we lived in different places and went to different churches.

Shopping in the loop was more fun if you got something before anyone else who wanted the same thing got it. One year I got the last box of pinecone incense that was the special at Woolworth's. It smelled wonderful, just like summer camp. Two other kids were crying about me buying it. I felt bad about it for a few minutes but then decided that if they had gotten there first, I would be the one crying. I learned that if you like something, buy it quickly since someone else will do it if you're not fast enough.

New Year's Eve came soon after we finished returning all the Christmas stuff that didn't fit. We had the first real party in our house. My sister and parents both invited people to the party. My friend, Gene, also came. It was a great time. I even saw my dad dance with some of the nurses from the hospital where my sister was working part time. One lady, Nell, danced several times with my father. They looked like they were having fun. I guess he was not supposed to have that much fun because after everyone went home, my mother screamed at him for dancing with her too much. Nell was not invited back to our house. That was too bad. She was nice.

Streets

The snow had finally melted and Easter was behind us. There were only a few more months of school left before summer vacation. Kasz had his dad help him build a street scooter. He used some paint he found behind the factory near his house to make it blue.

"It looks like a robin's egg," I told him.

"Very funny, let's see you do better."

"No, it's really good-looking, just bright."

"Yeah, well that's the only color they had back there and it's better than just some dirty brown box color."

"No, I like it. Can you help me put one together? I've got some old skates that Bonnie is throwing out."

"Let me look at them, the trucks have to be OK or don't bother building one."

"They look OK, see," I said, handing him the old skates. He nodded that they were OK.

"You got some two-by-fours and a good solid box?"

"Um hum."

"How about asking your uncle for a hammer, saw, and some nails? I got the rest of the small wood for handles and foot stoppers."

I asked Uncle Stanley for the stuff we needed. He gave them to me without asking why and closed his door. I guess he knew what we were building since he kind of squinted over at Kasz's scooter and smiled.

We spread the parts out in the gangway and started work. It must have taken us a few hours to cut the straight lines for the bottom board, pound lots of nails into the bottom of the box to attach it, and put on the handles. It started to look like a real scooter.

"Ya gotta line the trucks up even or you'll be going at an angle, no matter what you do," said Gene, who came over to watch what we were doing.

"How do you know?" I asked

"My dad helped me put one together on Sunday."

"So where is it?"

"Well, it's like this," he began.

A few minutes later, he was still telling us about building the scooter.

"Yeah, so where is it?"

"It got run over by the garbage truck."

"What? How did that happen? You only built it a few days ago," I said. "What was it doing in the street anyway?"

"I forgot to put it away after we tested it. I had it next to the trash-cans in the gangway. I went to school on Monday and Mr. Nowicki rolled them out to the street for the garbage truck to empty."

"Yeah, so how did the truck roll over it?"

"I guess he thought it was junk and put it next to the cans on the sidewalk. They mus'ta not seen it when it rolled under the wheels as they picked up the cans to throw the junk in the back. Next thing they heard was a loud crunch."

"Wow!" said Kasz."Good thing mine is blue, can't mistake it for junk looking like that."

"Could you save anything?" I asked.

"Naw, I guess they just threw all the splinters and stuff in the back and kept going."

"Boy, that's too bad. Well, you can use mine when we get it finished," I told him.

He smiled.

Rather than painting the box, I used the extra nails to pound bottle caps all over the sides. Nobody could ever mistake this scooter for junk!

Kasz and I took our new scooters into the street for a test ride around the block. Off we went down one side of the triangle, turned at the Dew Drop, then at the grocery store, and headed back to our house on the corner. Both scooters were perfect. Not even the bumps in the street made either scooter go on an angle.

My scooter lasted four days. Gene and I took turns using it. The bearings in the front wheels on the rear truck fell out and it stopped turning. That was it. Nobody had any old skates lying around, so we put the scooter in the basement to wait until we found some new ones. Kasz still had his working, but since only the small kids had scooters that worked, he put his away till mine got fixed. It was OK anyway since baseball season was starting and the Cubs were back in town.

———

Even without a ball field, we played baseball almost every day. If it rained we couldn't play ball but went to the Y.

If there were trucks parked in the dirt fields at the end of the street, we might not have a right or left field, depending on where they parked, but we still played. Sometimes a broom handle might take the place of a baseball bat, but we would play. It wasn't the Windy City sixteen-inch softball either. We played with the real thing, a regulation Rawlings official league hardball.

Wally was one of the neighborhood kids. His dad worked maintenance at Wrigley Field and always had balls that they were throwing out after practice games and stuff. Wally was real popular during baseball season. He had a withered right arm, but he always played OK in right field. It didn't hurt that without him nobody could play. He didn't get a hit very often. Not many people hit to right field anyway.

"Hey batter, hey batter, bet'sh strike out," the infield chanted to the fat kid at bat. He was from Gary and staying with his cousin Beverley who lived down near the Dew Drop. Someone said his name was Ignatius. We called him Iggy.

"Com'on pitcher, let's see what'sh got," he yelled back.

I was playing short, Kasz was pitching, and Gene was playing first. Kasz wound up and let it fly. Right down the middle of the plate. Strike one the catcher yelled. Iggy looked back at him and scowled, just like Randy Jackson would. Another pitch that he swung at tipped over the parked cars and flew into the gangway by Danuta's house. It bounced off the brick wall and landed in a puddle of water. It got back to Kasz soaking wet. He shook it off, wound up, and pitched.

Iggy connected with the ball and drove it straight toward me. I saw it come off the bat as it shattered into several pieces. I put my glove up as the ball came whistling across the street, bounced once just alongside of Kasz and just over the edge of his leather fingers. I could see it coming up off the street, but I just couldn't move. I watched it get bigger and bigger and then nothing.

I woke up with everyone standing around me. I was looking up into the sun.

"You OK?" Kasz asked.

"What?"

"You got hit by the ball. You all right?" he said, trying to shield my face from the bright sunlight.

"Yeah, I think so." I tried to stand up but got so dizzy that I had to lie back down.

"Why don't you lay there a few minutes; that was a really good hit Iggy got by hitting you. He made it to third."

"What? Yeah, that's too bad. Sorry I missed it." I sat up and touched my forehead. I had a pretty good-sized egg starting right in the middle of it.

"How about you go sit on the curb for a while. Stan will take your place, OK?"

I nodded and slowly got up, staggered over to a space in front of the Olds, and plopped down.

Iggy sort of smiled and said, "Sorry, thought you were a better catcher."

"Yeah, sure. I just missed it."

He smirked.

The game continued. I got dizzy and threw up between my feet. Nobody noticed. After the inning was finished, I told the guys I was going to go home to take a rest. They said, "See ya," and "Watch yourself, butterfingers."

I walked the two doors down to my house and slowly pulled myself upstairs. I lay down on the floor in front of the television. There was nothing on. I fell asleep watching the test pattern.

When my mom got home, I was still sleeping and dinner was not made. She was mad and shook me awake until she noticed the lump on my forehead.

I told her what happened. She made me take two terrible-tasting aspirins, get into my pajamas, and then into bed. The next thing I knew, it was morning and the swelling was down slightly. Good thing it was Saturday or I'd have to miss school. I was so tired that I couldn't get out of bed.

By Monday I was back to school but still moving slowly. It took me an extra ten minutes to walk to St. Boniface, and I was late for church. It was good my mom gave me a note for Sister Theon. She read it, looked at my head, and told me to just go sit in the back of the church until after Mass. She didn't get mad at me for being late. I started to think getting hit in the head was not such a bad thing.

On Wednesday, I was feeling like always, but I didn't want to play jump rope or hopscotch with the girls and especially not baseball with the guys. It took a few weeks before all the black and blue was gone from my forehead and I wanted to start doing stuff again. I watched the ball games from my window and didn't feel like going out there to do any running around.

Couple a weeks later Kasz and I played some catch in the street. I held the glove away from my body. I didn't want to take any chances on that ball hitting me again but it felt good to be playing ball again. By the time I was ready to get back into the street game, our season was put on hold while the Holy Trinity street carnival was being set up at the corner by the Dew Drop.

The Carnival was set up around Memorial Day. Not everyone could afford to go to Riverview or places like that, so the church set up games, rides, and food in the street. That side of the block would be closed for a few days while the rides and tents were there. For a nickel you could go on the merry-go-round, the whip, or ride some real ponies. Most of us played the games like ring toss, knocking over the dolls with a baseball, and breaking balloons with darts. They were the best. The food was not so good, but most parents spent their regular food money on that stuff because the church sponsored the carnival. We didn't.

Around the other side of our block, someone would always open a fireplug to give the kids a cool place to play on hot days. Water would gush out and sometimes a dad would get a plank of wood and put it in front of the opening to make a fountain. We all liked running under it. It usually took an hour or so until the fire department came and turned the water off. They always threatened to have whoever did it arrested but nobody ever was.

———

After Memorial Day, my parents thought that I should learn to ride a bike and got me one. There was lots of room in the street to ride around without getting hurt. Not many cars came through, and I could always stay on the sidewalk if it was busy with traffic from the factory.

It took a few weeks with my dad helping me to really get good at riding. A couple of the older kids already had bikes and were showing off riding with no hands. They could ride around the block, turning corners and all without touching the handlebars. They were really good. I started learning but was afraid of falling so I just did it coming straight, but I was very fast in the street.

I started riding faster and faster going around our block. I went around half a dozen times at full speed, hoping that my mom would be looking out the window to see how fast I could go. One day I was just passing our house when a car started pulling out of a parking place across the street; I had to swerve to avoid hitting the car. My mom saw that. She waved for me to come home.

I walked into the house, smiled, and said, "How did you like my riding? Pretty fast, huh?"

She stormed up to me, and I got such a crack in the face from her I almost fell over.

"Are you trying to kill yourself? What's the matter with you? You're riding like a maniac! If that's the way you're going to ride, I'm locking that bike up until you can learn how to behave."

"What did I do?" I wailed.

"Wait till your father gets home; he'll really give it to you."

He did. I didn't see the bike again.

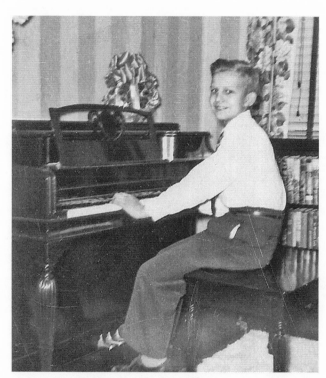

**Dickie stops accordion lessons and tries the
piano-It didn't work either.**

Dickie and a friend in Humboldt Park.

Eigth grade class at St. Boniface

Back room at pharmacy after the robbery

Dickie and his dad at graduation from St. Boniface.

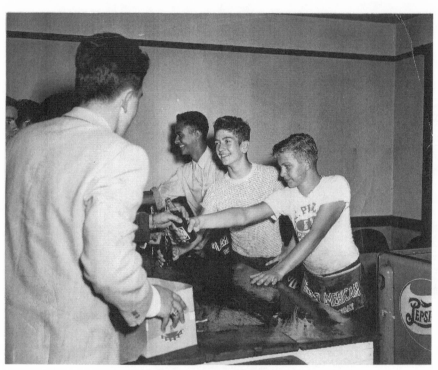

Dickie helps out at a school party.

The Movies

I love the movies, not the mushy ones but the detective stories, war pictures, and Westerns. I could watch them all day long. On lots of Saturdays I did. On other days the Y, which was right next door to the theater, was where I spent the day. Both were great places but the movies were better, unless it was an old one.

Saturdays were special days, not like holidays, but different from school days. I mostly went to the neighborhood movie theater so my parents could get stuff done without me. For twenty-five cents, you could see three movies, twenty-five cartoons, and three serials at the Division Theater. For another twenty-five cents, I ate popcorn, hot dogs, and drank pop all day. Sometimes Kasz, Gene, and I would split stuff and get candy, but it was usually too sweet for us to eat all day.

There were a few kids from over near Chicago Avenue that used to sneak into the Saturday morning programs. One kid would get in line to buy tickets and then go right into the theater and open the fire door behind the screen. Three or four kids would run in and then close the door quickly before the manager saw what they were doing. Those kids could buy more popcorn and stuff with the money they saved by not paying for tickets.

One time so many kids tried to do it that the manager turned on the lights after the first movie and made everyone show their ticket stub. If you didn't have one, out you went. No questions asked. Sneaking in stopped for a few Saturdays after that, but it always started up again. I never tried doing it and neither did the other kids from our neighborhood.

The people who ran the theater were not always happy to have the place filled with kids caus there was lots of running around, shouting, and throwing stuff. Sometimes the old guys had to turn on the lights in the auditorium when popcorn and bigger things were thrown from the balcony. They 'specially didn't like water balloons falling down from the balcony. I only got soaked once. Playing tag was OK when the boring parts were on, but usually there was enough stuff happening on the screen that we sat still most of the time.

I was dropped off at the theater by my mom or dad just as the 8:45 a.m. ticket line was starting, and I would walk home about six o'clock bleary eyed, excited, and hungry. Getting out the large metal tub after dinner and taking a bath usually calmed things down as we got ready for church on Sunday and maybe another movie with my mom and sister. They liked movies almost as much as I did.

There were five movie theaters near Throop Street that we went to and maybe a dozen more in the loop. They changed their programs three times per week; new big movies were on Friday, Saturday, and Sunday. The not so good ones were Monday and Tuesday, but the really bad ones were Wednesday and Thursday.

Going to the movies was important if you wanted to win any of the sidewalk games like Sky Blue.

"Marlene Dietrich, Diana Durban, Paulette Colbert, Betty Grable, Barbara Stanwick, Bette Davis, Clara Bow, Pola Negri, William Powell, and Marjorie Main," Bonnie chanted while going up and down the chalk-marked boxes on the sidewalk without stopping.

"Tom Mix, Gene Autry, William Boyd, Lash Larue, Humphrey Bogart," I stuttered, stopping at the top before turning around. I hopped up, turned, and began again. "Sydney Greenstreet, Richard Widmark, William Bendix, John Wayne, Jimmy Stewart, and Jimmy Cagney," I shouted following her.

On and on it went until someone ran out of names they remembered from watching the latest movies. Since you couldn't use a name more than once you needed to know lots of them. I usually lost; there were more girl actresses and I didn't know their names as well as the boys.

We also went to lots of Wednesday night movies because of the dishes. The Biltmore, Roscoe, and Hub were regular places to go regardless of what was playing. They gave away free dishes with every ticket you bought on Wednesdays and Thursdays. Some of the theaters gave them away on Tuesday also, but each theater gave away a different pattern of the dishes so you had to keep going to their movies, not another place. I liked the ones with bunches of wheat and ribbons along the edges of the plates. The set with the brown solid lines around the edge were pretty ugly.

I guess that giving one dish at a time every week forced you to keep coming back to get a complete set. It did with my mother and aunt. Getting the dishes was the most important thing. To get each of the place settings, all of us had to go. Sometimes we even brought my grandmother, who sat and slept, just to make sure we got a complete set of dishes that week. Other times we went three nights in a row to get a sugar bowl, creamer, and serving plate that matched the set. Kids tickets didn't count, but my mom didn't want to leave us alone at home so we had to tag along.

The movies weren't as important as getting the dishes—that was until the Victor Mature movie came out. My aunt said a picture of my grandfather in his coffin was actually in the show.

"See," she said. "It's the same picture from Olecicz's Funeral Home," holding up a big photograph.

I looked at the photography of one of the dead gangsters in the movie and thought about my grandfather. They looked the same to me.

"They need to pay us for using Pa like that," Aunt Mary told my mother.

I heard them argue back and forth for weeks but in the end, nothing happened. The movie was a flop and nobody got any money. I did watch the movies more closely after that; hoping to spot someone else from our family so we could get money for them being there without someone saying it was OK. It never happened again.

Going for dishes during the week was kind of like going to work for my mom, Aunt Mary, and their friends. But going to a loop theater was a dress-up time for everyone. There seemed to be hundreds of theaters downtown to choose from. We never went during the week because it took too long to get there. Buses did not run so often after nine o'clock, so we usually went on Saturday afternoon or Sunday morning after church.

The first show at the Chicago, State & Lake, Oriental, or McVickers often had movie stars come to the grand opening of a new film. We might stand in line for hours to get good seats close to the stage to hear them sing, tell jokes, or just talk about the movie. I saw the Three Stooges at the Oriental and Lucille Ball and Desi Arnaz singing and playing the conga drums before *The Long, Long Trailer* started. Lots and lots of times, no matter how long you waited in line, you never got in. Either way, there was usually an ice cream sundae, root beer float, or milk shake waiting at one of the soda fountains that dotted the loop.

Movies were the place kids learned about the world outside the neighborhood. It was a place where the good guys usually won; people lived in great houses; they wore swell clothes and ate fancy food; they drove big, fast cars; and they always got the best girl. It always paid to be honest in the movies; the bad guy usually went to prison or was shot by the good guy. You always wanted to wear a white hat playing police or cowboys after the movies. Nobody wanted to get shot all the time or be in jail.

My dad didn't like going to movies very much. He kept talking about them not being safe.

"I go all the time, they seem safe to me," I told him.

"They're not fireproof, even if they say they are."

"What can burn? Nobody I know smokes in the theater, except maybe in the lobby."

"They have fires all the time. Did anybody tell you about the Iroquois Theater fire here in Chicago?"

"Uh uh, what happened?"

"Six hundred people were burned to death near the loop about fifty years ago. The building was supposed to be fireproof."

"That was really bad, but we have fire doors and everything now. Something like that can't happen anymore"

"Well, always look around when you sit down and know where the exit is, all right?"

"Yes, sir."

A few weeks later, the Oakley Theater over on Chicago Avenue blew up. My dad said they thought it was a gas leak in a heater. Only one person was killed.

I guess bad things did happen at the movies.

After the Oakley explosion, all of us started going more to the bigger theaters and cut down our visits to the neighborhood ones where we usually went. We just started going to the places like the Biltmore, Congress, Portage, Logan, and Harding. They were really big, had beautiful lobbies, and big concession stands. I even thought their popcorn was better.

Since television was starting to have more and more programs that were fun to watch, I wasn't as interested in spending a whole day sitting inside a theatre looking at a bunch of stuff that wasn't that good just to see one good movie. Television was making it much easier to enjoy stuff at home.

Holidays still were centered on seeing the newest release from Hollywood. Dinner might be special, but everyone was always checking out the time to make sure we would all be at the theater early. Sometimes there would be television holiday programs that competed with going to see a new film. There were even a few times that my mom and sister wanted to go to a movie and I wanted to watch something on television. When that happened, they went and my dad and I stayed home and watched television programs.

"Which do you like better?" he asked one Christmas when we were home alone.

"I like them both," I said, pointing at the screen. "But watching these programs are easier. All I have to do is push the button and turn the dial."

"But, what about the movies, don't you want to go see the new, big pictures?"

"Sure," I replied, "but not as often. I can see lots of good stuff right here, without getting cold or walking seven blocks or taking the El to the loop."

"I sure wish they would hurry up and get the rest of those dish sets they're trying to fill in before the movies go out of business. These television programs are going to replace them soon."

"I hope not, I really like things on the big screen. It's a lot more real; television is kinda in between radio and the movies. Radio lets you decide what people look like and the places they are talking about. The movies show you everything they think is important. The television makes big things small and that's how you remember them. They don't seem as real or as important as when they are on the big screen."

"It's like a lot of things," he said. "You have to decide how you want to be entertained. Size makes a difference in how you enjoy it."

"Well, I guess I like all three ways; it depends on what it is I'm going to see."

"Um hum."

"But, I guess movies are still special to me. I think they always will be."

"OK, but remember life is not always like the movies; in fact, most of it isn't. Remember which is which."

Schools

I went to five different schools before finishing the eighth grade, one each in Michigan and Florida and the rest in Chicago. Except for first grade in Michigan, they were Catholic schools. All kind of the same but slightly different. At some the nuns were nice, at others they were like my Aunt Mary. They yelled and were always ready to smack you. Since my parents moved around a lot, I learned a bunch about both.

The one thing that was the same everywhere was church. You went to mass every school day and couldn't understand a word except for the sermon unless you spoke Latin. When I got old enough, at St. Boniface, I signed up to be an altar boy. I thought if I understood what the priest was talking about at the altar, I might like it better. Most of the time it was just plain scary and not a friendly place.

The Sisters kept telling us that Jesus loved us, but most of the stories were about bad things that had happened to people and Jesus was always trying to fix them. If not that, bad things were happening to him that he let happen without fighting back. It was kind of hard to figure out.

On Wednesday afternoons we got out of school early so that kids from the public school could come for religion classes. They called it CCD classes, and it was for the non-Catholics to learn about Jesus. We had an extra hour to play while they were using our desks. We usually didn't play with kids who were from public school, except maybe at the Y, but it was OK for them to use our classrooms when we weren't there.

Sometimes our schools would take students who were not Catholic. It was usually to help them with a problem. My dad told me about a Jewish kid that was always causing trouble at public school. His father decided that since Catholic schools have strict discipline, having him attend a Catholic school might straighten him out. The first day he was there, he behaved 100 percent better than he had at any of the other public schools he had attended. After the first week of extraordinary behavior, his father asked, "What happened? You've changed. You seem like a different person since you've been attending Catholic school."

The kid said, "Well, the first morning, the principal took me to the classroom, pointed to the crucifix hanging on the wall in the front, and said, "See what happens to Jews that don't behave."

"I didn't want that to happen to me."

———

I thought that being an altar boy was like being a junior priest: we would learn some of the secrets. The problem was that I had to learn Latin to learn if there were any secrets worth knowing.

"Ad Deum qui laetificat juventutem meam," was the first of the forty-four Latin responses that altar boys had to learn in order to serve at mass. It took six months in seventh grade to learn them backward and forward. Sister Theon, the principal, tested us.

We worked every day after school memorizing one section of the Mass at a time. By Christmas we were ready for our test. I passed the first time and then assisted another altar boy who had served Mass for over a year. By Easter I was ready for my first Mass alone.

"You have six o'clock Mass on Monday with Frank," Sister Theon told me. "Make sure you're there on time."

"Yes, Sister," was all I could say. I was frightened that I wouldn't get it right.

It went fine until just before the end of the school year. She caught Billie and me talking while we were serving at seven o'clock Mass one Saturday. We didn't see anyone in the church but she was like a crazy person.

"How can you disrespect God, the church, Father Rockaszewki, and me like that? Shame on both of you! Both of you are done here, no more serving mass. I'll be sending a letter to your parents. You'll both be lucky if you don't burn in hell. If I could expel you from school for this, you would both be gone on Monday," she wailed. Father Rocky didn't even notice that we had said a few words while serving him. He told her to calm down; we did no harm to God.

94

My dad said he thought Billie and I had set a record for the shortest time ever served by altar boys. He was not upset. My mother was another story. Sister Theon convinced her that I was what she called an instigator, whatever that was, and deserved to be severely punished. My dad didn't let that happen. He said the Latin I learned would be good in high school. I didn't have to go to church early every day either. It was their loss, not mine.

It was about this time that we were learning about the dignity of labor in school and all the different jobs that you could get. One that I thought was really great was truck farming. Sister Francis told us all about how they brought fruits and vegetables to Chicago. She told us that it was good work in the clean, fresh air and not too far away from our neighborhood. I was all for working there.

"Sister?"

"Yes."

"How do they grow them?"

"Grow what?"

"You know, the trucks, there's lots of different kinds? What kind of seeds do they use?"

"What are you talking about?"

"The trucks, if it's a truck farm, how do they grow the trucks? From seeds or what?"

Everyone laughed.

"Come up here, right now," she snapped from the front of the room.

"Can anyone explain to him what a truck farm is?" She looked around the room.

"Frank, let's start with you."

"Well Sister, I kinda wondered about that myself. Why call it a truck farm if they don't grow trucks? Doesn't make sense."

"Sit down! Mary, what about you?"

"Yes, Sister," she said with a smirk.

"Truck farm. It is a farm devoted to the production of vegetables for the market." She sat down.

"Do they grow trucks?"

"No, Sister."

"Where do you get these ideas?" she said, shaking my arm roughly.

I shrugged and pulled away from her.

"Stop causing trouble, go sit down."

I did as she said, but I still thought growing trucks was a great idea, much better than pulling potatoes out of the ground.

Right after the truck farm lesson, Sister told us about the school wide spelling bee at the end of the week. The winner would get a new dictionary.

"Why does the winner need a new dictionary?" whispered William.

"Maybe they should get a new prayer book," I answered quietly.

"Why? A dictionary sounds good."

"If they win the contest, they already can spell. But I'll bet they used up all their prayers asking God to help them win. They probably need some new ones; a prayer book would help them."

William laughed. He told Billy who told Sue who told Constantine and soon the whole room was laughing.

Someone told Sister. She did not laugh. Instead she gave us a lecture on good behavior, deportment, and how to study for the bee.

To Sister's surprise, and mine, I won our class competition. I was one of three in the school finals. I lost trying to spell the word *cerulean*. I never heard of it. They said it was a kind of blue color. Frank from the other eighth grade classroom won. He always won. Sister Francis must have been impressed that I could do something right. On my report card, she wrote: "Does not always work up to his potential." I guess that was a compliment for doing well on the bee. Frank got the dictionary, not a prayer book.

The end of the school year meant that everyone would be moving up a grade in the fall unless you were in the eighth grade; then you had graduation. In our school, eighth grade usually meant final exams, a class presentation in front of all the other students, and a graduation cer-emony. Exams were supposed to cover everything you learned during all eight years in school.

Testing usually took place a few weeks before the end of the year. You were supposed to really study for them; otherwise you might get held back another year. We had Albert in our class. He got held back the last year. He was always getting into trouble. I hoped he graduated with us; he was a lot older and not many of the kids wanted to play with him.

After school one day close to graduation, I told my mother, "I need a dark blue sport coat, powder blue slacks, a white shirt, and a dark blue tie for graduation."

"What? Just for one day?"

I nodded.

"Oh, and blue suede shoes."

"Sister Theon says the boys are getting off easy. The girls' outfits look like wedding dresses."

"You sure she's going to let you out of there? I don't want to buy an outfit if she's going to hold you back. She isn't, is she?"

"Is what?"

"Going to hold you back."

"Don't think so."

"I'll wait until next week to make sure you're really getting out of there."

"Don't wait too long; they'll sell out of those pants quick."

"I don't think you need to worry. Powder blue slacks are not big sellers, except maybe at your school."

Practice for graduation was not a big deal. We only had to practice three times before Sister Theon was satisfied that we could march in a straight line down the main aisle and get back and forth from our pews to the front of the church and back to our seats. She read off our names from the altar to see if we could respond by getting up and walking forward to collect our graduation certificate when we were called. Everyone, including Albert, got it right, much to Sister Theon's surprise.

The really big deal was getting our class presentation ready for the assembly on the last day before school ended. Every class was supposed to do something for the school, but the eighth grade was expected to have something really special. We had nothing two weeks before we were to go on stage. Frank was supposed to be working with Sister Francis to get either a singing or dancing program for us.

"All right, let's do it once more," Sister Francis shouted while moving between the rows of us trying to walk through the dance.

We moved back-to-back, arms up and down, up and down with the music blaring and squeaking on the loudspeaker. "Cuckoo, cuckoo da

97

da de da da da" filled the room over and over. We were supposed to be like little windmills moving in a field of tulips.

"This is kid stuff! Why are we doing this dance? The fourth graders should be doing it," I told Kathleen, my windmill partner.

"Sister Theon is mad at this class so she gave Frank this program for us to do," she said over her shoulder.

"The Cuckoo Waltz really is for little kids. I don't want to do it."

"Why don't you tell her you don't want to do it?" Kathleen giggled.

"I will!" I said, and I did.

She listened to me, and then said she agreed. We needed a few special things in our program to show that we were ready to graduate.

"Thank you for telling me," she said. "Since you wanted something more mature, I think I want you to recite a poem for the school. Something from the classics! Yes, Let me think for a moment, Ah-yes, Shakespeare. That's what you need to recite. William Shakespeare."

"Shakespeare? But I don't know any of his poems. We never even read any of his poems in class."

"I'll leave it up to you to choose any of his works. If you expect to graduate from this school, I had better hear one of his poems from the stage next Friday."

"I'm going to be held over for sure," I told Kasz after school. I explained what happened with Sister Theon.

We walked to the library to look up William Shakespeare's poems. There were thirty books with them.

God they were long. I'd never be able to memorize one of them for next Friday. My mom is going to kill me; I'm never going to get out of eighth grade.

Kasz looked in one book while I looked in another. After about five of them, he poked me. "Look at this," pointing to the page in front of him.

I looked at what he was talking about, read it again, and said, "Kasz, you're the best friend anyone could ever have."

The following Friday we had just finished our Cuckoo Waltz when Sister Theon pointed to me and said, "It's your turn."

"Our final presentation will be a poem by William Shakespeare," and she waved me onto the stage.

I walked slowly to the microphone and began:

"Where the Bee Sucks, There Suck I" by WILLIAM SHAKESPEARE
Where the bee sucks, there suck I:
In a cowslip's bell I lie;
There I couch when owls do cry.
On the bat's back I do fly
After summer merrily.
Merrily, merrily shall I live now
Under the blossom that hangs on the bough.

By the first line, the auditorium was howling with laughter. It took a few minutes to get everyone quieted down. There were lots of sucking sounds for the rest of the day. Sister Theon was not happy. But she checked and found that I did what she asked. No more, no less.

I graduated. I was pretty sure she didn't want me around anymore.

Playing in Alleys

Alleys were the best places to play and we had lots of them. The best one was along Milwaukee Avenue just before it emptied onto Division Street close to Ashland Avenue. There were lots of factories, stores, a second floor bowling alley, and a magic shop that faced Milwaukee Avenue. Close behind it was the alley to the west of Milwaukee Avenue. It had several stores and warehouse that sold herbs, medicines, and chemicals. Behind the stores we could find great stuff almost every time we went junk picking.

The best time to find good treasure was in the winter. Stuff usually had no smell then. We never did it in the summer. The rats were too big and scary. There were also lots of bums walking around when the weather was nice and we didn't want to be around them. In the winter they moved over toward Maxwell Street so nothing was picked over before we got to it. We had everything to ourselves. It was safer.

None of our parents knew we were looking through junk in the alleys. If they did we all would have been beaten or at least yelled at a lot. They thought we were playing street ball, at the Y, or hanging out by the grocery store on the middle of my block. We didn't need to look for junk; our parents all worked and we had enough to eat. It was just exciting. We usually had to hide the stuff we found.

One of the stores had displays of small animals in the window. There were squirrels, chipmunks, and a few white foxes in make believe winter scenes. I didn't know what they sold but there were always bits and pieces of fur, dried skin, parts of frogs, and guts wrapped in old newspapers behind that store. My younger cousin, Ken, liked to go through the guts, but the rest of us didn't want to go on that side of Milwaukee Ave. There were too many good things on our side of the street, but sometimes I had to go with him. If my Aunt Mary ever found out that we were taking him picking, I would be beaten for sure. If I didn't let him go where he wanted, he would snitch to her about what we were doing.

Once the bowling alley threw out a few sets of pins that were chipped and cracked. We used an old wagon we found behind the factory across from my grandmother's house and brought twenty-eight of them back to my house. We put them behind the furnace next to the basement rooms where my uncle Stanley lived. Of course he found them and yelled at me for bringing "that shit" home. The next day he said that he threw them out while I was at school. He did it before we could find a way to use them so nobody was too mad at me for losing them. I really thought that he found a way to trade them for a pint of liquor.

―――――

Instead of going to the Y after school one day, we decided to go picking. Within twenty feet of where we started, we found a big pile of boxes and bottles.

"Boy this bottle is heavy," Kasz said, holding up a dark brown bottle he found in some cardboard boxes.

"Let me see it," I said.

It was really dark brown and even smaller than the glass cream bottles the milk truck delivered to our house. It held maybe a little more than a Coke bottle but was much heavier. I shook it and it felt like there were weights in the bottle moving back and forth each time I turned it in my hand.

"I wonder what's in it," Ken said.

"I don't know. Let's open it and see," I said, twisting open the black, hard-plastic cap.

"Wow, it's silver!" we all gasped.

"We're rich," Ken shouted, jumping up and down.

I held the bottle up so I could look at the smudged, dirty label. All I could see were the letters *Hg* and some language that I couldn't read after it. It didn't say anything that looked like silver.

"I don't think it's silver," I said. "It's *Hg*. Whatever that is."

"Let's see if it pours," said Kasz.

"Yeah, let's see," said Ken.

"All right" I said, tipping the bottle slightly so some of the silver stuff poured out onto some cardboard on the ground in the alley.

I poured slowly. The liquid silver plopped out and quickly became round balls that rolled across the flat surface of the cardboard. They glistened and then they flowed all over onto the alley bricks. I tried to scoop them up before they got away from us. They oozed into my hand, formed back into a puddle, and then plopped back into the bottle.

"Wow!" everyone said.

"That's really something. Do it again!" they cheered.

I poured it out again, but this time into a cardboard box that had sides on it. I thought that the liquid would stay in the box and not run out onto the bricks. I was right.

"Can I touch it?" asked Ken.

"Sure, just don't get it dirty," I said.

He stuck his fingers into the puddle and stirred it around. When he took his fingers out, a fine sliver powder stuck to them. He wiped them off on his trousers and licked off what was left.

"I don't think you should put your fingers in your mouth after touching this stuff," I told him. "Maybe it's poison or something."

"Nah, they wouldn't throw poison out in the alley," Kasz said.

"I don't know, maybe they didn't know it was being thrown out. Maybe we should ask them."

"You want to go to their door and tell them you were picking their trash and want to know if they threw out the Hg bottle?"

While we were talking, Ken pulled a penny from his pocket and dragged it through the puddle of silver stuff in the box. The silver stuck to it, so he started wiping it off with his fingers. It polished the penny and made it look like a shiny silver coin. Kasz had a nickel and did the same thing. Both had really bright coins, but their fingers turned black.

"Don't put your fingers in your mouth again," I told Ken. Kasz nodded in agreement.

"What is this stuff?" they asked together.

"I don't know, but I don't think we should have it," I said.

"Who can tell us what it is?" Ken asked.

We were close to the Division Street YMCA, so I suggested we go there and ask Mr. Teske. He knew everything and would not tell our parents we were trash picking. The Y was only a block from where we were. Mr. Teske ran the kids section of the Y and was a really good guy. He was also in the building all the time. Sure enough, he was there when we trooped down the stairs into the kids section.

"Can you tell us what this stuff is? We found it kinda behind the bowling alley over on Milwaukee Avenue," I said. Ken and Kasz stood behind me.

"Let's see what you have there, Dickie," he told me while taking the bottle into his big hands.

"Hum, exactly where did you find the bottle?" he asked, looking up from the tattered label.

"In the alley off Division that runs behind the magic store and bowling alley, right there between them, in some boxes, by the trash barrels," I told him. Ken and Kasz nodded in agreement.

"Why don't you guys go get a shower and take a swim, I'll tell the checkers that you are OK to go to the head of the line, right now."

We looked at each other and said, "Sure. Thanks, Mr. Teske." We ran to the locker room, stripped down, and were in the hot showers within minutes.

An hour later, clean but with uncombed, damp hair, we were back in Mr. Teske's office. There was another small, thin man with him when we rushed into the office.

"Boys, this is Mr. Martin, he owns Marco Chemical Company. That's the company whose bottle you found in the alley. It seems that it was thrown out by mistake. It is very valuable and very dangerous. He is very grateful that you found it and brought it to me."

"Boys," Mr. Martin began, "I want to thank you for bringing this bottle here. You could have been really hurt if you didn't do that. I'm really happy to have it back."

"What is Hg?" I asked him.

He frowned and looked at Mr. Teske, then he said, "It's a chemical called mercury. Sometimes it's called liquid silver."

"Yeah, that's what it looks like," said Kasz.

"You're right," said Mr. Martin. "But, it's very dangerous to handle without special equipment. You boys didn't touch the liquid did you?"

We all looked at each other and Ken said, "I did, I rubbed it on my fingers and then put some coins in it. I licked it off my fingers."

"I poured some in my hand," I volunteered.

Mr. Martin looked troubled but said, "Since it was only once and for a short time, it's probably OK. You were lucky to have come here and cleaned up right after you did that. You should thank Mr. Teske for getting you into the pool right away. I don't think you'll have any problems, but please don't touch anything you find outside my factory ever again. If you see anything, knock on the door and ask for me. Don't touch it."

"Yes, sir," we all answered.

"Good, good, boys. I also talked to Mr. Teske and we agree that a little reward is in order for you doing the right thing and bringing this bottle to the Y," he said, holding up the brown bottle.

We wondered what kind of reward he was talking about, but he continued, "I have a brand new silver dollar for each of you," he said, handing each of us the large coin. Mr. Teske shook each of our hands and told us that we were following the spirit of the Y by being honest and bringing the bottle to him. We could hardly believe our luck: a silver dollar each. Both men shook our hands again. We filed out of his office and started for home clutching our coins.

"Are we lucky!" Kasz said.

"We sure are," Ken added.

"How are we going to explain having a silver dollar to our parents?" I asked.

"We can just spend it; we don't have to tell them about it," Ken offered.

"Yeah," added Kasz.

"I don't know if that will work. If you spend the money in the neighborhood, someone will tell your mom that you had money and she will come after you," I said.

"They'll never find out," Ken whined.

"I don't want to get a beating for something good that we did," I said.

"Well, what are you going to do?" Kasz asked me.

"I'm not sure yet. Look, we need to get home for dinner or we'll get in trouble right now. Can you hide the money until tomorrow?" They both nodded. "OK, let's talk about it after school. Remember, don't show it to anyone or try spending it until then. All right?" Both nodded their heads.

We all grinned and nodded to each other. It was quite a day. We split up on Noble and Milwaukee Avenue and each of us walked home in different directions.

We met after school the next day in front of the hot dog stand.

"Well, what are we going to do?" Kasz asked. Ken nodded.

"I already took care of my dollar," I said.

"What did you do with it?" they asked together.

"I took it to church this morning and put it in the poor box," I told them.

"You what?" they said.

"I gave it to the poor. We were lucky getting it and would have a hard time spending it. They need it more than me," I said. "Besides, I don't want to get another beating from my dad if he was thinking I was stealing money from someone. Would you believe the story about getting a reward for trash picking if you were our dad?"

Everybody nodded to each other.

I thought about the last time I got a beating for taking money without permission.

We split up for the day but agreed to go trash picking again right after school the next day.

———

We started at the other end of the same alley where we found the Hg. Within a few minutes of poking around behind another factory, we opened a huge box that was filled with glass beads used to make necklaces and bracelets.

They were the most beautiful things we had ever seen. We took turns carrying the large, heavy box back to my house and up to the back porch. It was filled with piles and piles of beads; strings of red, green, gold, silver, turquoise, purple hearts, and dozens of other colors: round, oval, long, fat, short, square, and oblong beads that could be strung together. They spilled out over the stairs and floor.

My other cousins from downstairs, Bonnie and Josephine, saw them and ran to tattle on us to my aunt. She came out of her flat and started to yell at us but stopped when she saw what we had all over the place.

It turned out that our parents were thrilled when they saw what we had found. They didn't ask too many questions about where we got them after we said they were "in the alley, near the Y."

Within a few hours, all the beads were in the hands of neighbors and relatives. The strands were nicely wrapped up as gifts. At least for the rest of the day we were treated the way we thought hunters coming home with a deer over their shoulders might have been in a Jack London book. It felt pretty good.

Ken and Kasz put their silver dollars in the poor box at Holy Trinity the next day. They didn't want to press their luck either.

Lessons

*T*arzan swung across the wild river. He leaped from tree to tree and escaped from the lion that splashed into the water close behind him. It was swept away in the fast current. He made one final dive for the riverbank.

I let go of the rope and dropped onto the pile of tumbling mats we had pushed on the roll-around rack to the center of the gym floor.

Kasz quickly grabbed the rope and was already running to start his long swing across the floor into another corner. I had to rush to get in the right spot so he could fly through the air and land safely. If I didn't get there, he would let go anyway and probably break something.

It was Saturday morning, just after the Y opened and nobody else was in the gym. Maybe the rain kept everyone home this morning. We decided not to go to the movies but spend the day at the Y.

The lights were still out so it was kind of scary with the rain hitting the windows on the second floor alongside the running track.

"Don't move those mats," Kasz yelled.

"OK, come ahead," I shouted to Kasz, who was still climbing toward the second floor.

"Wow, look at that lightning," he said just as the thunder roared next to the building.

He fell.

"You all right?" I asked

He just lay there on the pile of mats looking at the ceiling. His eyes looked buggy and his mouth was open but nothing was coming out.

I got scared.

He groaned, "Oh my God, I thought I was going to die."

"You OK?"

"That was really, really scary but fun," he said, rolling onto one elbow and looking at me. "You try it."

"Try what?"

"Climb up as high as the track and let go."

"Are you nuts? You almost killed yourself and you want me to try it?"

"No, really, it's great."

"I don't think I want to do that. Swinging is great but falling two stories onto a mat is not something I want to do today."

"Come on, you scared?"

"Look, we have Family Night on Monday for the Leader Corp and I'm supposed to be in it. I want to be there in one piece."

"Scaredy cat, scaredy cat," he started chanting.

"Quiet down before Levi or one of the other leaders comes in here and finds us rolling the mat around without any supervision. They'll run us off."

Kasz stopped the yelling. We went back to playing Tarzan and Jungle Jim.

It was probably ten o' clock before the lights popped on and people started filing into the gym for basketball. Levi was surprised to see us swinging and the mats moved from their normal resting place.

"How come you guys are in here?" he asked me.

"The door was unlocked so we thought we'd play until it was time to swim."

"How long you been here?"

"My dad dropped us off about eight forty-five."

"You've been here about an hour and a half?"

Kasz and I looked at each other.

"I guess so. We didn't hurt anything."

"That's not the point. You, Dickie, of all people should know that there is supposed to be a leader or supervisor here when you use the gym."

"Yes, sir."

"So this morning you thought it was OK to be in here without any-one around rolling the mats and swinging on the rope?"

I looked down.

"You're supposed to get your Junior Leader 'L' on Monday, aren't you?"

"Yes, sir."

"Well, I think we need to have a talk about that since you should know better than what I'm seeing here."

I didn't know what to say.

"Before you go home today, I want you to stop by my office."

I nodded dumbly to him. Kasz and I walked out of the swinging doors and continued down to the Boys Department.

"I'm in real trouble now," I said to Kasz.

"What's the big deal?"

"I come here every day after school and have been learning to be a Junior Leader. Monday is to be a demonstration for our parents of what we learned and a ceremony to get our 'L'. My mom is supposed to buy me a white uniform so we can all look the same for the program."

"So."

"He might not let me be in the program because I broke the rules about playing without supervision. If I had my mom buy a uniform that I won't use, she is going to kill me."

"Talk to him, maybe it's not so bad."

"I've been at three summer camps with him. He knows I shouldn't have been playing Tarzan. What if you had gotten hurt?"

Kasz looked away.

***

It was crowded and busy as we hurried down the narrow stairs to the Boys Department. We got into the line for the eleven o'clock swim. We stayed for three sessions and were dressed and walking out at one thirty.

I forgot about getting yelled at by Levi.

Levi was in charge of the Youth Program and worked for Mr. Teske. He was a really great guy that taught all our classes and ran the Junior Leader and Leader programs during the year and Camp Channing during the summer. I did not want to disappoint him.

After swimming I saw Levi walking back to the locker room. Kasz also saw him, waved to me, and said, "See you, good luck," and headed for home.

Levi and I walked to the small program office. He closed the door.

"I'm really disappointed in you, Dickie. You know the rules about playing alone with the equipment."

"It's my fault, sir. Nobody was there. It was dark and rainy and things just got going, I didn't think."

"You know why we have those rules? Right?"

"Yes, sir! So nobody gets hurt." I told him about what Kasz had done.

He listened and said. "That's exactly why we don't want anybody doing things that are not properly supervised. Both of you are lucky that he didn't break anything."

"I know, I thought he was dead."

Levi put his hand on my shoulder. "You learned a good lesson today. Fortunately Kasz was not hurt while you learned it."

I said nothing.

He turned me to face him and put both his hands on my shoulders.

"When you give your word that you will do something the right way, you are supposed to do it. You didn't do that today, did you?"

"No, sir! I'm really sorry, I just forgot." I started to cry.

"Stop crying," he said softly. "The important thing is that nobody was hurt and you learned your lesson. Didn't you?"

I stopped sniveling and nodded my head.

"'Body, Mind, and Spirit' are not just words on the Leader Triangle. They really mean something. Doing the right thing even when nobody else is around is what sets a leader apart from everybody else. Always remember that."

"Yes sir, I'll remember."

"OK, get out of here. I'll see you Monday evening. Are your parents coming?"

I smiled. "My mom for sure; my dad if he gets off work on time."

———

My mom was later than usual getting home on Monday. The program was to start at seven o'clock and she got home at five thirty. I needed to be at the Y by six thirty to get ready for the program.

"Did you get my outfit?" I asked her when she came in the door.

"Here it is," she said, handing me a Marshall Field's bag.

I tore it open and froze.

"Where is the rest of it?" I asked her.

"It's all there. Just what you asked for: shorts and a shirt.

"It all supposed to be white," I told her.

"I know, you told me, but they had these great shorts on special. I'm sure the Y will love them."

———

At seven thirty, twenty of us lined up to show what we had learned in the Junior Leaders program. We did cartwheels, back flips, bounced on the trampoline, threw medicine balls, and worked every floor apparatus the Y owned. People were yelling and shouting about how great we were doing everything.

When we were finished, Mr. Eugene Levendosky, "Levi," made a speech thanking all the parents for coming, raising such great young men, and began presenting the Junior Leader awards to all of us. He told our families that he was proud to work with such a good group that had mastered so many skills. He handed the Ls to each boy in the group.

When he got to me, he said, "I want to present this L to Dickie. He is one of our really great junior leaders. He would be even better if he had on the same uniform of everybody else." He laughed.

I laughed too, standing there in my white shirt and chartreuse shorts.

Too bad my dad didn't get to see me standing there.

Television

The white enamel corner-mounted sink had one leg and a dark blue chip out of the finish on the upper left corner. It looked like someone hit it with a hammer or something hard. My Saturday morning job was to clean and polish everything in the kitchen. There was one brass faucet on the sink that needed to be polished once a week; otherwise, it made everything look old and dirty. If I rubbed it hard enough with Babo and steel wool, it would shine. I never could get the blue to go away or the chip to get smaller. I was not supposed to clean behind the curtain under the sink. It covered the drain, water pipes, and the cleaning stuff my mom kept on the floor.

The radio made the work go faster, especially programs like *Grand Central Station* and *Let's Pretend*. I finished the sink and cleaned the stove before their episodes were even over. I didn't even notice doing the work while listening to them; I was part of the story. Somehow the work got done without even thinking about it. Each program began when the announcer said the train was "diving into the two-mile tunnel under Park Avenue" and then the conductor called "Grand Central Station." The story began each time with "Grand Central Station, crossroads of a million private lives."

Radio let me be inside the story imagining the places, like New York, that they were talking about. Everything was inside my head. I was standing there watching the actors. It was my program, my story. Cleaning the sink was something I just did while it happened.

"Get your work finished unless you don't want to get to the Y today," my sister yelled.

"Almost done, it's still not even nine o'clock. One more program and I'll be finished."

"You better be. Mom will be home from the bakery so if you want any Pączki, hurry up."

"Who died and left you boss?"

"Listen mister, just get your stuff done. I don't want her getting mad around here. I want to go out today."

"Yeah, yeah, I'll be done in a few minutes."

"She'll be here soon so get busy."

Those still-warm Pączki were great even though my sister was angry because I got the jelly one she wanted. My mom really liked the way the faucet shined.

———

When television started having programs on Saturday morning, I didn't want to do anything but watch what was on. The programs I wanted to see were downstairs at my Aunt Mary's house. The stories were now outside of my mind, inside a small box with a screen. It gave me a picture of what it wanted me to see or think about. Getting chores done was not so much fun anymore. I got yelled at a lot and for a few weeks Aunt Mary wouldn't turn the television set on until after all the chores were done. Nobody was happy, but the radio programs were still there for us to listen to.

"It's Howdy Doody Time, it's Howdy Doody Time," was the song I heard every school day downstairs from my Aunt Mary's house. They had the first television set in our neighborhood. It was a huge Du Mont. The screen was about six inches square. They bought one of those magnifying attachments that made the picture almost a foot wide. It was really something to see. Most days she let me watch with her kids.

"*Kukla, Fran, and Ollie*," I shouted, "or *Captain Video*."

"I don't like that show," Bonnie yelled, joined by Kenny and Josephine.

"How 'bout *Tom Corbett—Space Cadet*? He's pretty good."

"That's OK, it's a good one!" said Kenny, but the girls screamed even louder.

"Aunt Mary, can't we watch something good?" I whined.

"Sure," she said and turned the set off. "Read a book or get outside and play."

"See," Bonnie said. "Can't you be happy and just watch something without complaining? Now we get nothing."

I went outside to look for Kasz. We played until I had to get home to make dinner. Bonnie had to stay home and help clean the house; boy was she mad.

My parents got our first set about six months later. It was a big Zenith that stood on the floor with a twelve-inch round screen.

Right after we got it, I kind of stopped going out after school for a few weeks. We would rush home and lie down in front of the set and start watching. If I had to make dinner, I would stick my head out from the kitchen and watch while things were cooking. For a while we even ate in front of the set instead of at the table. The programs were really swell. Even the commercials were good.

Changing from listening to the radio to watching on the television did not take long, except for some stuff. Friday nights the Gillette Cavalcade of Sports had things that weren't on the television. Sunday night was also radio, as the *FBI in Peace and War, X minus 1, Mr. and Mrs. North, Lou Diamond; Private Eye, Duffy's Tavern*, and *Amos 'n' Andy* were on. Television couldn't compare to them. Also, when the television set stopped working, getting it fixed was a problem. If you had to wait for new tubes, the radio still had pretty good programs.

Our television set had lots of tubes in the back. They controlled vertical hold, horizontal hold, and picture on and off. There was a chart that told you which tube to pull out and replace when it stopped working right. You had to take the back off the set with a screwdriver and pull out the hot tubes without breaking off the pins inside the plugs. If that happened, you needed a repairman. They charged ten dollars just to come to the house. Your parents would beat you if something got broken back there. Ten bucks plus parts to come and fix it was lots of money.

"OK, I'll go down to the Apteka and get the tubes. Better give me five dollars," I told my mom one evening after the picture went black.

"So much? Make sure you get the right ones," she said, putting the ones I pulled out from the back of the set into a paper bag.

I took the bag and money and walked the three blocks to the store. "I need these tubes," I told the kid with glasses working at the drug store on the corner of Milwaukee and Noble.

"Let's see if we have them," he said and opened the cabinet under the test station with all the plug-in places for different-sized tubes. He squinted inside and pulled out some boxes.

"Looks like I got two of the three you need. You want I should order the other one? Might take a few days to get it."

"Nah, I'll take the two now and try over at Wally's for the other one." My mom was not going to wait three days to watch Liberace.

"OK, let's see...that's two dollars and eighty-nine cents for those two," he said. I counted the change.

Another stop and I had everything and even some change left over. It took about half an hour.

I needed about another ten minutes to replace the tubes before I could turn on the set. We waited while it warmed up, watched as the picture slowly stopped flopping over and over and finally stopped moving. The *Lucky Strike Hour* had already started and the dancing packs were still on the stage as the picture came into focus. Once I was sure it was working OK, I closed up the back and replaced the screws to hold it in place. My Uncle Joe just left the back loose on his Du Mount to save time replacing tubes.

"Uncle Milty," I said as my mother started changing channels, "Milton Berle is really funny."

"I don't like him. We're watching *Cavalcade of Stars*, then that nice Polish boy, what's his name?"

"Liberace?" I said, making a face.

"Right, and his brother?" she said without noticing my look.

"George, I hate him too. Both of them are boring."

"He's Polish, you need to support him," she said, glaring at me.

"He dresses funny, what's the matter with him?"

"He's an artist. You should play the piano as well as him."

"I don't want to play the piano; I want to watch wrestling or bowling."

"Go listen on the radio in the bedroom if you want sports that much. I'm watching Liberace."

She always won. If Liberace wasn't on, she would tell me to turn on some guy called Lawrence Welk who played polka music. He was even worse.

———

115

My aunt and uncle on the south side told us they bought a big new Admiral television and invited us to see it. One Sunday morning we drove there to visit my Cousin Walt, watch their new set, and have dinner. We went early so Walt and I could play and read his comic books while the test patterns were still on. He had thousands of them, because his dad worked at the newspaper loading trucks. He also brought home the newspaper comics for the next month before they went into the Sunday paper. It was neat, but it would ruin Sunday mornings for the next month.

He always gave me some stacks of comics to take home. There were Blackhawk, Sgt. Slaughter, Superman, Batman, and lots of horror ones I never saw before. But the best thing about getting there early was their new television. It was huge.

It was Sunday morning and when the national anthem was over, we watched the Lone Ranger. Aunt Polly told us something about the William Tell music that played while he was riding his horse across the prairie as it was starting. Walt said it was the Lone Ranger's theme song. Hoppy was also on before the baseball game started.

The picture was really clear, not much snow. Wow, who would go to the ballpark if they could watch it at home with a big television? I know I wouldn't.

My Uncle Fred was a big man. He drove a delivery truck and loved sports. He was always betting on games and drinking beer. When we got there about ten o'clock, he already had a few empty beer bottles on the kitchen table. The Cubs game was supposed to start at twelve thirty, so we had to finish dinner before it began. He was a White Sox fan, but they were out of town so it was OK to watch the Cubs.

By the time we sat down to dinner, Uncle Fred was yelling at Aunt Polly and threw a couple of beer bottles at her in the kitchen. He was drunk and missed.

Walt and I had to pick up the glass and sweep up the floors.

My mom finally said, "We have to go," to Polly.

I picked up some of the comic books Walt gave me. Fred was storming around the house yelling at everyone and he tore the pile out of my hands and started mumbling to me about stealing his stuff. My mom said to leave the comics and we left. We stopped at a restaurant for dinner at some place with black-and-white tiles on the floor and good chicken soup.

I got home early enough to find Kasz and Gene playing some catch and joined them.

"Thought you were going to see your cousin today," said Kasz.

"We did. Came back early."

"See the game?"

"Nah, we stopped at a restaurant to eat."

"Isn't your uncle a big White Sox fan? Did he watch the Cubs?"

"He started to, but he fell asleep before it started."

"Well, anyway, the Cubs won four to one. Heard it on the radio; sounded like a good game."

"My dad wouldn't turn on the car radio. Too much traffic he said. Can't concentrate on driving with all that distraction."

We played until almost dark.

"Well, better get in before my mom starts yelling for me," I said. "Last week of school coming up, don't want to sleep late in the morning."

"Yeah, sure can't wait till next Friday. We're supposed to go to Riverview as a school outing."

"Riverview, really? Wow, I should go to your school," I said.

Gene nodded.

Kasz just grinned. He knew it was really special that his school was going there.

"Wish we could go with you."

"Yeah, well I got to study for our tests this week," I said. "My mom says that if I don't stop watching the television, my grades are going to get even worse."

"Yeah, my ma says that too," said Gene.

We had some sandwiches and Campbell's tomato soup for dinner and watched some new program called *You Are There*. Mom and Dad said that it was educational, so I wasn't that interested in it. It had something to do with Mexico and a revolution. They interviewed some general who had one of the prisoners in front of him. He kept asking the soldier, who was tied to a chair, question after question but never got a response. The general turned to the camera and said, "I'm sorry, I should have told you that this peasant could not answer me because I already had his tongue cut out." At that moment the peasant opened his mouth and started howling.

"Now that's pretty good," I said.

"What's the matter with you?" my mom said and scowled at me.

"Leave the boy alone; that's the way they did things in Poland, too. He needs to learn how the world works," my dad said.

"That's real?"

"What, you think everything is like here in America?"

"Well, isn't it?"

"Maybe this television is better than radio. It shows you, not just tells you, about how things are in other places."

I looked back at the television set.

"Can I watch Jackie Gleason or maybe wrestling tonight instead?"

Working

In our neighborhood when you were old enough to work, you worked, no exceptions. Any job that paid you was OK. Money was money.

Kasz and I were in the alley behind the bowling alley on Milwaukee Avenue trash picking one afternoon when the back door opened. One of the bartenders stuck his head out and looked around. He squinted in the sunlight but saw us looking through some boxes behind the bead shop next door.

"Hey kids, needa make some money?" he shouted to us. "One'a my pinsetters ain't coming in today. I need someone to help out. You guys wanna work?"

"Sure," I answered before Kasz could start to ask questions.

"OK, get in here right now. I got a league starting in about twenty minutes. I'll show you what to do."

"Come on, Kasz," I said and started to follow the big, dirty-looking guy through the stairway door. "It should be fun."

"I need to be home by dark," Kasz whined.

"How long can a bowling game take?" I said as we climbed the stairs into the dark bowling alley. They were just opening and the alley lights were not on yet.

"You guys ever work setting pins before?" the bartender asked.

"I watch it on TV," said Kasz.

"It's a lot different than that," he said laughing. "Come on in back of the alley and I'll show you what to do."

He showed us how the racks worked and how to get the pins set up for each frame. Getting the balls back up the lanes was easy even if the balls were kind of heavy.

"Each of you take three lanes, I have a few other guys coming for the others."

"OK," we said.

"Get ready, the bowlers get here in about ten minutes, and it will be very busy for three or four hours."

Kasz and I looked at each other. Three hours would mean we would be late for dinner; four would have our parents out looking for us. A beating would probably follow.

"Maybe if we work fast, we can get done sooner," Kasz suggested.

"I don't think it works that way. The bowlers throw when they're ready, we don't have anything to do with it."

"I'm going to get a beating for sure," he moaned as we rolled up our sleeves and got ready to start. The other guys came in to set up the alleys next to us. They hung up their leather jackets and stuck rolled cigarette packs into their T-shirt sleeves.

I stopped watching them and jumped out of the pit when I heard my first ball coming down one of my alleys. Pins went flying as the guy got a strike. It took a few minutes for me to get the pins back in the rack and reset them for the next throw. I was hardly out of the pit when another ball was rolling in the next alley. While I was doing that, both of my other lanes exploded with flying pins and balls hitting the backstop. Kasz was having the same problem. The older guys in the other alleys didn't seem to be having any problems as they jumped back and forth between balls. They even had time to light up cigarettes while they were racking up the pins.

After racking up dozens of pins and sending balls back to the bowlers, my arms started to get sore.

"Hey Kasz, how ya doing?" I yelled over the noise of strikes and balls rolling on the alleys.

"I'm getting tired. How 'bout you?"

"How do we get a rest?" I yelled to the skinny guy with the DA haircut next to me.

He laughed, "No rest until the beer frame; that's in about twenty minutes. Keep on rackin' 'em up. You don't want Jimmy to get pissed off at you."

"Who's Jimmy?"

"The guy who hired you. Screw up his league night, and he'll beat the shit out of you," he said, jumping out of the way of the next ball.

"Kasz, we're in trouble. We need to get out of here," I yelled.

"What's wrong?" he asked.

"At the beer frame, we run for the back stairs and get out of here. My mom will kill me if I'm late getting home."

"You can say that again."

We lifted pins, returned balls, reset racks, and learned to jump out of the way of fastballs. Bowling looked like fun on television but from behind the pins, it was really hard work.

After what seemed like a year, the balls stopped coming toward us. Kasz and I looked at each other. We picked up our jackets and walked along the top of the pits past the older boys who were smoking and telling dirty stories. We got to the end of the pit, opened the bowling alley door, and ran to the back stairs. We almost flew down to the first floor, pulled open the slide bolt lock, and ran into the alley. It was already dark. I pulled the door closed just as I heard someone heavy running down the stairs.

"Run," I yelled to Kasz, and we both took off down the alley toward Milwaukee Avenue. I heard Jimmy yell, "You little bastards, if I see you again, I'll cut your little balls off and hang 'em up where you were setting pins. Little pricks."

We split up at the next corner. Kasz went toward Paulina, and I went straight home. I got there just in time to see my dad walking up the front steps of our building. I ran up and walked inside and up the stairs next to him.

"Kind of late, aren't you?" he asked.

"Yeah, I was playing with Kasz and we forgot to check the time. Sorry."

"Well, try to be more careful next time."

"Yes, sir," I said but was thinking, *I'll be careful that Jimmy doesn't see me on the street. I don't want him cutting parts off me.*

I saw Kasz the next day after school.

"Was your mom mad last night?"

"Nah, she was OK, hardly noticed when I got back. She was watching the TV, hav'n a beer."

"My dad was OK with it too, hardly said anything 'bout it."

"No more working for guys like Jimmy," I finally said. "Next time I take a job, I need to get paid before I start work. My arms are still tired."

One of the first real paying jobs I had was working in the coat check-room at a Polish wedding. The bride's father gave out all the jobs. My sister was in the wedding party, so two of us kids were asked to take care of the coats. We split the tips.

It was winter in Chicago and everyone had long coats, hats, and rubber boots. Each item had a claim check and we could set our prices anyway we wanted. The wedding hall was on the second floor over a bar on Division Street, near Damen Avenue. The coatroom was at the top of the stairs, just before you went into the big hall that looked like the auditorium at St. Boniface School but without seats.

Everyone had something to take off. We made lots of money that night. We also lost lots of stuff until we figured out how to use the claim check tags.

"Gimme my coat, the black one over there," slurred the bride's brother, pointing to the rack nearest to the door.

I looked at the tag he gave me.

"That's not your coat, this one is," I said handing him the one with his number on it.

"I want that one too," he said. "It's for Tad, you know, the best man."

I nodded, "You have his tag?"

"No," he said slapping his pockets. "No tag."

"We can't give out coats without the tag. Your dad told us, 'No tag, no coat.'"

"But that's his coat," he said, pointing at the wall that had a hundred black coats hanging on it. "I know it's his."

"Ask him to bring the tag," I said.

He reached into his pocket. "Oh, here it is. I found his tag," and handed me a five-dollar bill.

Billy Wisnewski, who was maybe fifteen, was working with me. He grabbed the bill and said, "Yes sir, that's your coat. Thank you," handing him the one he was pointing to.

"Hey, you can't do that. We're going to be short a coat later on."

"This your first time working a coatroom, right?"

I nodded.

"Don't worry 'bout it. By the end of the night, nobody will remember what they wore here anyway. Always smile, take the money, and thank the people for it."

"But they'll have the wrong coats."

"They'll also be very drunk when they come to get their stuff. If it doesn't fit right, it won't make any difference. Do the best you can, OK?"

"OK," I said, watching the room fill up with people dancing, drinking, and moving to and from the banquet tables overflowing with food. I could hardly hear anything over the band it was so loud.

We didn't have much to do after the last of the guests checked their coats, so we took turns getting something to eat. Billy even let a few of the young couples close the window to the coatroom for a few minutes at a time if they paid him a buck while it was quiet. They could get about ten minutes alone unless someone came for a coat.

"What are they doing in there?" I asked Billy.

"They're necking."

What's that?"

"When you get older, you'll find out. For now, just take the buck and close the window. Make sure you knock before you open it up if someone comes to get their stuff."

I made three dollars before someone came. An old couple walked up and asked for their coats. I forgot to knock and opened the window too quickly. The last couple that went in about five minutes before was on the floor, on top of some coats, kissing. The girl was kind of sitting on top of him when the light shone in the window. She jumped up, pulled down her skirt, and ran out wiping at her lipstick. The guy grinned at me, winked, and strolled slowly out. The old couple looked mad for some reason, grabbed their stuff, and walked down the stairs. I had to ask them for a tip. They wouldn't talk to me and just left.

It was funny because when the girl went home with her parents, she sort of smiled at me like we shared a secret. Maybe we did, I wasn't sure.

It was really late when my parents came in their car to get my sister and me from the wedding party. Billy had to stay to the very end to make sure everybody had all their stuff and close up the room. We split everything that we collected up till then.

"Thirty-eight dollars and fifty cents is your share," said Billy. "I'll give you half of whatever else I get before closing."

"Nah," I said. "If I'm not working, why should you give me the money?"

"'Cause that's the deal. Half of everything for the night."

"That's OK; you keep it after I go. You'll earn it."

"I'll save it for you, if you change your mind later."

"Don't worry, I won't. You earn it, you keep it! It was fun working with you."

"OK, see you around."

"Why didn't you take the money from Billy? He was ready to give it to you," asked my Dad.

"I won't be here to work. Why should he pay me for doing nothing?"

"That was your deal, wasn't it?"

"Yeah, so? I'm going home early with you. He has to do all the work."

He thought about something for a minute then said, "All right, let's just go home."

It was really cold at midnight. I was tired but felt good. I made more money in a night than lots of people made working in a week.

"Wish I could make money like this every day," I told my dad. "Thirty-eight dollars and fifty cents. Oh, I forgot I have another six dollars that I forgot to share with Billy from renting the room. I need to go back and give him half."

My dad stopped the car and turned to me. "Renting the room?" he asked. My sister looked sideways at me.

"Yeah, you know, for letting kids use the room to be alone together for a few minutes during the evening."

"You rent the coatroom to kids?" he scowled.

"Sure, Billy does it at all the weddings where he works. He makes lots of extra tips that way."

"I think that this is the last wedding you should work at if that's what goes on."

He turned to my sister, "Do you know anything about this?"

124

She shook her head and gave me a really dirty look. "No," she answered.

"Well, I would hope not. If giving the money back to Billy would do any good, we would be going back there right now," he said. Then he added, "I think that we need to give at least half of what you earned to the poor box. You can't spend it."

"What, you want to give my money away? Why?"

"You don't take money to help people commit sins. That's not what they teach you at school, is it?"

"No, but I wasn't doing anything, they were just being alone together in the room. What's wrong with that?"

He paused and looked at me. "For right now, all you need to know is that what you kids were doing was wrong and you are not going to make money from it. Take half or I'll take it all for the poor. Which do you want?"

I lowered my head. "I'll take half, but I still don't understand why you are doing this."

"When you get as old as your sister, you will," he said, looking at her. She lowered her eyes.

I shook my head but had no idea what was going on.

"Someday you will," he said, smiling slightly. "Someday you will."

Cortez Street

W est of Ashland Avenue people looked different, dressed better, and shopped farther north on Milwaukee Ave. My parents wanted to move there. The neighborhood around my grandmother's house was old, tired, and like many of the others on our block, mostly wooden. Only stores, schools, factories, and churches were made of brick or stone.

My family and I stayed at my grandmother's for three years after my father's sundry store closed up in central Florida. We lived on the second floor in one of the buildings owned by my buscia. We only had cold water. Taking baths on Saturday in the tin bathtub was not as good as showers at the Division Street YMCA. We had to heat the water on the kitchen stove.

There were lots of kids around to play with when my parents let me out of the house. I had three cousins who lived downstairs from us. We played lots of games in their house until one of the kids pooped under a bed when we were playing hide and seek and didn't tell anybody till their mom found it. She beat all of us with a belt and said we had to play outside even if it was forty below zero. Living there was not always so great.

Everyone always worked, except my uncle Stanley: he drank whiskey, slept a lot, and cursed at my grandmother. He was supposed to keep the yard clean and the pipes working, but he did neither very often. "Hire someone else to do your shit work, I'm not doing it," was something he yelled almost every day, when he was sober enough to think about what he was supposed to do.

My job was to cook dinner for our family. My sister came home from Holy Trinity High School about four thirty, my mother from Marshall Field's about five thirty, and my dad from school and then the Standard

Club in the loop about seven. I was supposed to be home at three thirty to get meals ready, but I sometimes stopped to play and was often late getting them started.

Meals during the week were usually some type of meat, potatoes, canned vegetables, and white bread. Sometimes buttered noodles or Minute Rice would take the place of potatoes.

My mother had something called anemia. She was supposed to eat liver once a week and drink Malvas malt liquor every day. She preferred calf liver, but beef liver was also OK for her. I learned to make both. Pan fried with butter was my mother's favorite, but my dad liked it fried with onions. So did I.

My aunt who lived downstairs from us taught me to make noodles with ketchup. It was not very good; sometimes you would gag on the stuff. I also watched her make chicken soup, stuffed cabbages, and hamburgers; boil hot dogs and kielbasa; and fry kiescka. Except for the stuffed cabbages, everything was pretty easy to make. Learning kitchen tricks from her let me have extra time to play with my friends, so getting home right after school was not so important.

One time I stayed at a friend's house until after five. Going home I saw my mother getting off the bus on Milwaukee Avenue on her way home. I ran through some shortcuts across the neighborhood and had dinner cooking before she opened the door. She never knew that it only took a few minutes to get everything in the pans and the table set. Fortunately, my sister was at some special event at school and got home even later than my mom did, so I didn't get caught.

My parents wanted to move to their own house and on weekends would go on what they called house-hunting trips. I went to the Division Theater on Saturday morning to watch the twenty-five cartoons, three movies, and three serials while they hunted.

One Saturday they picked me up after the movies and took my sister and me to look at our new house on West Cortez Street. It was the only wooden house on the block. All of the other two- and three-flat buildings were made of brick or stone. Our house had four apartments. We were going to live on the first floor, in the front. Everyone had their own bedroom. There was one bathroom with a tub and shower.

"You the new kid from twenty-six twelve?" asked the chubby boy sitting on the front stoop of a two flat down the street.

I looked up at him and said, "Yeah, we're just moving in,"

"I'm Davie," he said. "My mom and I live here, downstairs, in the back."

"I'm Rich."

"Are you?"

"Am I what?"

"Rich," he laughed.

I laughed along with him and said, "No, I don't think so, but I have my own room."

We both laughed.

Davie took me around back of the building and into his house. It looked worse than my Uncle Stanley's basement apartment after he had been drinking for a long weekend. There was junk everywhere: bicycle parts, newspapers stacked in piles on the floor, and dirty dishes on the one-legged enamel sink that might have been white at one time. There were lots and lots of empty beer bottles on every table, window ledge, and all over the worn linoleum floor. Wow, was it a mess. Davie didn't seem to notice the jumble of stuff all over the place. He walked to the kitchen table, pushed some dishes to one side, and pointed to a rickety chair for me to sit on.

"I build things," he said, pulling a sprocket from a Schwinn out from under some dirty clothes on the floor. "I'm putting a bike together, you need a bike?"

"I don't know yet, maybe," I said.

"Well, I'll give you a good deal when you want one. Everybody comes to me when they need things."

"What kinds of things?"

"Anything you need, Davie can get it for you."

"Ah, OK, great," I said.

It felt really dirty in the apartment just sitting there. I wanted to leave but was not sure how to do it without getting Davie mad. He seemed kind of touchy about stuff, and he was tall as well as having a big belly. I liked being alone with him less and less so I said, "My mom sent me to the store and will be wondering where I went if I don't get home soon."

"How much money did she give you?" he asked.

"Enough for some milk and bread."

"How about we go to the store together? I'll take the stuff for you and you can just give me the money."

"You mean take the stuff without paying for it?"

He laughed, "Sure, why else would you give me the money?"

"I don't think that's a good thing to do."

"Are you chicken?"

"It's not right. I think I'd better get going now," I said, getting up from the chair.

He blocked my way. "Listen Dickie, I'll let it go this time, but you better think about who your friends are in the neighborhood." He smiled and said, "See you around."

He walked into what was probably his bedroom and closed the door. I almost ran out of the apartment and the half a block to the store.

We also had lots of special people on our block. There was Ruffy Silverstein, a professional wrestler, who I'd seen on Saturday Night Wrestling; Mrs. Wisnewski, who did something called electrolysis in her apartment; John, who owned the meat market and grocery store and the tavern, lived across the street; Mr. Syple, who owned a drugstore, had a Packard Caribbean convertible that he parked on our block. It was the most beautiful mint-green color. I loved it.

On the next block west of my house was the public school. It was much bigger than St. Boniface School and its church together. It was three stories tall and had lots of playgrounds and two softball diamonds. But the best part was that the other kids in the neighborhood told me "it had screens that looked like chain-link fencing on all of the windows and lots of ledges, on all four sides of the building." I wasn't sure why the screens were a big deal until I played our first game of IT at the school.

For my first game, I was IT. The rule was that you covered your eyes for a count of sixty then went looking for the other kids. It took me a few minutes to look up rather than around the playground to find them. Sure enough, they had climbed up the ledges and screens and were laughing at me from the second- and third-floor windows and ledges. I had to climb up and try to tag them while holding on with one hand, and the toes of my sneakers stuck into the holes in the chain links. It was pretty scary. I thought playing softball was more fun.

A few days after I played my first game, there were lots of fire trucks down at the school early one evening.

"What happened?" I asked one of the kids I knew from playing IT.

"Wally fell from the third floor."

"How is he?"

"They think he broke his leg. He fell on the lower roof. They said he was lucky. If he had fallen on the sidewalk, he might have been killed."

"Wow," was all I could say. Wally was a skinny kid and the best climber on the block; he was like a monkey on the screens and ledges.

About a week later, there were signs all over the building. DANGER: NO CLIMBING.

Wally was climbing again by the end of the summer.

By then, I also thought there was no better place in the city to live than my block, except for Davie.

Davie always seemed to turn up when I was going to the store, a movie, or Humboldt Park to fish. My mom heard from some neighbors that Davie was in reform school before we moved into our house. He started a neighbor's garage on fire after they caught him trying to steal the spare tire from the trunk of their car. His new favorite game was "follow the leader."

When Davie asked you to play, you played.

Almost all of the houses in the neighborhood had garages that lined the alleys either behind or alongside of them. "Follow the leader" often meant that we raced around the block while jumping from roof to roof, climbing down telephone poles, and clambering over garbage cans to get back on roofs on the other side of the alley.

The last time I played, Davie had a surprise for us. He raced ahead, jumped down from the roof behind his house, and disappeared. We were all standing on his garage roof yelling for him to come out when what looked like a fireball raced past us in between Davie's garage and the one belonging to Mr. Syple.

"What was that?" I yelled, just as the wild screeching began.

"What's that?" yelled Gene, holding on to his Cubs ball cap and pointing down between the garages.

"That's Davie's cat, and its tail is on fire!" he shrieked.

"Holy crap!" I yelled. "Davie, what are you doing?"

Just then Davie appeared from the doorway to his garage with a squirt gun that had fire dripping from the barrel. "Just trying out a new invention," he said. "This is the fire gun," he said, pulling the trigger and shooting a ten-foot long streak of flame toward us on the roof.

"Are you nuts?" I yelled, jumping back. "Someone could get hurt with you doing that."

"Nah, I only shot the cat in the tail, and he ran off to stick it in some water. He'll be OK. I didn't try to hit you guys."

"Well, why don't you put out the fire so we can keep playing?" I said.

Just then, a Chicago police cruiser turned into the alley at the end of the block and saw us on the roof. They turned on their red light and hit the siren. A fire truck was right behind them. We were too afraid to run, so the police took our names and told us to go home, except for Davie.

All our parents were called to the police station the next day. The police told them that Davie's cat had run off and set two garages on fire trying to put out the fire on its tail. Davie went back to reform school and we were told never to play on garage roofs again.

I decided to do more fishing. It was much harder to get in trouble with a fishing pole.

They put the cat to sleep.

To be honest, we did try Davie's invention again after he went away to reform school. We filled a squirt gun with Ronson lighter fluid and lit the tip. It did shoot a flame ten feet once in a while, but mostly it was only six or seven.

Worms

Our new yard had grass. My old neighborhood did not have anything green except a few small trees. There was grass in the park across from St. Boniface School but nowhere else. A few of the buscias had small boxes outside their windows that sometimes had a flower or two sprouting in them. At the end of the summer, there might be some tall weeds next to the railroad tracks and sunflowers might pop up just before school started around Labor Day. But grass we saw at Camp Channing, around houses we passed in the bus getting there, and in magazines and movies.

We moved from my grandmother's house just before I graduated from St. Boniface and the yard in the new place was just turning green. The front yard had sunshine on it and the grass there was bright. The backyard didn't get much sun because of the three-story apartment buildings on either side of our house. Having an alley alongside one side of it let air into the yard but not much sunlight, except around noon.

Very little was growing back there. It was mostly dirt. I was looking at it when my dad walked out into the yard.

He stopped, looked around, and said, "You will be responsible for the yard. There's a lawn mower in the basement, and I'll buy a hose so you can water things."

"What am I supposed to do?"

"Keep the grass green and cut it when it gets too long."

"That's it?"

"Well, the backyard needs to be dug up and some grass and maybe a few trees planted."

"You want me to dig up the yard and plant grass and trees? When am I going to do that? I still have school."

"There's time after school. It's good exercise," he said, walking back into the house.

Maybe we should have stayed at my grandmother's house, I thought. *I'm going to be Jonny Appleseed here.*

After school on Monday, I worked at getting the yard cleaned up before I could even think about planting anything. There was junk all over the place just under the top dirt. Old cans, nails, and bottle caps along with old tree roots were what I found the most. It was hard work.

"Did anyone ever clean up this yard?" I asked Mr. Wojtera, one of our renters that lived in the back of the building overlooking the yard.

"Never seen it," he said in broken English.

"Didn't think so."

"Nothing will grow in back, not enough light," he said. "Needs lots of light for grass."

"Tell my dad; he wants grass back here."

"You should play accordion, not plant grass," he said. "I teach."

Between the two, I would rather dig in the dirt.

My parents didn't; they thought it was a great idea to learn the accordion but still wanted the grass. Now I couldn't get away from either problem without someone knowing what I wasn't doing.

"He needs lessons three days a week and lots of practice," he told my mom. She agreed. I had nothing to say about it.

Karl turned out to be OK, but the accordion was another matter. I'm not a big kid and the accordion seemed twice my size. I had to sit down to play it.

I had a friend, Rickey, at St. Boniface who took lots of lessons until his accident.

His teacher told him to play a song with his small band for a school assembly. Rickey was standing on the stage holding this giant accordion when he started tipping forward from the weight. Before anybody could grab him, he fell forward into the first row of students. He wasn't hurt, but the accordion was totally wrecked. Rickey had a new nickname: "Tippy." I didn't want to repeat what happened to him. I also didn't much like accordion music. I don't know who had to pay to fix the wrecked accordion. I sure didn't want to do it!

Karl played violin, cello, accordion, and clarinet and he practiced every day. He was also a painter and had lots of his oil paintings all over the walls of their flat. He had five of his wife, Lennie, when she was younger that showed her naked. They were pretty good.

They were DPs that came to Chicago right after the war and were still waiting to get their citizenship. Lennie worked as a receptionist in a restaurant near the loop and Karl gave music lessons and played in an orchestra. My mother said she heard that they were Polish but worked for the Germans during the war and had to get out of Poland or else they would be killed.

She told my dad and me that Lennie was laughing about being a bit heavy but not like when she was in Germany during the war. Lennie said, "I didn't get out of bed one time for a month. I was so busy that I only ate chocolates the officers brought me and slept in between their visits. I couldn't get back into my dresses. It was OK, though; they bought me some new ones."

I wasn't sure what they were talking about, but I guess my parents didn't think too much of her after she told them about her life during the war. I guess Karl was OK because he just played music for dinners and stuff; he didn't have to fight against us.

"Don't look at those paintings of her either while you're taking lessons," my mom added. "She's nothing but a tramp. Even if she is older now."

I thought tramps looked pretty interesting without their clothes on.

————

Once a few weeks after we were in the house, we went to visit the cemetery. We stopped at one of the flower shops near St. Adalbert's on Milwaukee Avenue and bought three small evergreen trees. Two looked pretty scrawny sitting in the middle of the front yard, and the single one in the back was worse. But we had trees.

Every apartment building and house on Cortez Street had a small garden area between the sidewalk and the street. The one in front of our house was dirt like the rest of the yard. Next door to the west of us, there was a beautiful flower garden and a big tree. Every other house had grass, trees, and flowers all mixed up together. People were always watering, cutting, and trimming their gardens, except when snow was covering everything.

By the time I graduated from eighth grade, the yard was pretty well cleaned up but no grass was growing, even after my dad and I put down bags of grass seeds. It came up in some places but mostly the yard remained dirt covered.

My music lessons were much like the grass. Being hopeless at music was good. After a few months of scales and a wheezing accordion, Karl finally told my parents that it was a waste of time for me to continue. I looked like I was sad to get the news about my lack of musical ability but I couldn't wait to turn in my music sheets and start playing softball and fishing over at the Humboldt Park lagoons. The only thing I would miss was seeing the oil paintings.

———

I walked over to Humboldt Park for the first time a few weeks after we moved into our house. It took about twenty minutes to get over to the closest lagoon. There were a few adults and some kids younger than me fishing. I watched them for a while then went up to three young ones and asked, "What kinda of fish you catch?"

"I got a sunfish," the smallest kid said.

The others started pulling strings of small fish out of the water to show me what they had been catching. They said they were bluegill, crappies, and even one really ugly catfish. They had fishing poles that looked like long sticks with string and red-and-white bobbers on them. Only the oldest boy had a rod and reel.

"What do you use to catch them?" I asked the oldest boy.

"Bread is OK for the small fish, but you need either special dough or worms for the big ones."

"Dough, what's that?"

"Get your mom to give you some flour and mix it with bacon fat and a little water. You roll it into small balls. It sticks to the hook. Fish really like the taste. Kinda hard to make but works real good," he said while showing me how to put it on a hook and cast it into the water.

"What about the worms, where do you get them?"

All the kids laughed.

"What's so funny?"

"You live around here?" the older one asked. The other boys giggled.

"Yeah, just moved in over on Cortez near Rockwell."

"You got a yard?"

"Sure."

"Dig a hole and pull some out and put 'em in a can. They're all over the place."

"Really, I been digging in my yard all the time, haven't seen one."

"They're there," he said, lifting up a coffee can full of big, fat earthworms. "Look at these."

"These from your yard?"

"Nah, from next door, but I scoop them up all over the neighborhood. People don't mind you taking them. Really, they're all over the place."

"OK, thanks. I'll look for them when I get home."

"Ah, don't look for them now," he shouted to me as I was walking away.

I stopped. "Why not now?"

"They only come out at night. If you wait until after it rains or someone waters their yard, they're all over the place."

"Thanks. See you 'round."

That night I decided to go looking for worms on our block.

It was getting dark about eight thirty, and people were all sitting outside and talking. Kids were running around playing on the sidewalks. They didn't play as much in the streets here as by my grandmother's house—too many cars coming through. We also had the schoolyard on the next block. But more important now was how many worms were outside waiting to be caught.

"I got a can," I told my dad as I was leaving the house. "Be back when I get it filled," I added, expecting to be out for quite a while.

I used an old Cub Scout flashlight to look in the garden area next door. Nobody paid any attention to what I was doing.

"Find any?" came the shout from the front stoop next door. "Should be lot's over on the street side."

I walked in between the parked cars and the iron railing that surrounded the garden. "Don't see any," I answered.

"They're there; keep looking," the voice said. "Kids get 'em there all the time."

"Don't listen to him," another voice said loudly. "Haven't been any in our yard in years. Next thing he'll be sending you on a snipe hunt out in back," she laughed. "Get down the block; they have lot's down there."

I heard her say to the other person, "Don't tease the boy. What's the matter with you?" Then the door closed and I couldn't hear any more.

I walked quickly down past where I had talked with Davie right after moving in and stopped a few houses further down the street. I turned the flashlight on the garden and jumped back.

"Oh, my God," I stammered. The yard was a twisting tangle of big pink, red, and brown worms. They covered the grass, were under the flowers, and were dripping over onto the sidewalk. I'd never touched a worm in my life. Now there were thousands of them waiting to be put into my can. I reached for one but stopped short.

I had never touched a worm before.

Even at camp, I never went fishing; there was always lots of other stuff to do. I kind of stood there looking at the twisting piles of worms moving around and tried to think how I was going to get them into the can without touching them. *Maybe I could scoop them up with the can without needing to feel them.*

I guess I was gone longer than my parents thought was necessary because my dad came up behind me and said, "Did you find any?"

I pointed my light on the pile and said, "Take a look."

"Well, get them and let's go home," he said, pointing to the squirming pile.

"I can't, I've never done it before."

He paused, bent down, and picked a big earthworm from the pile and turned to me.

"Give me your hand."

I held out my right hand. He gently placed the squirming thing in the middle of it. It was cool and dry, not slimy like I thought.

"What does it feel like?" he asked quietly.

"Aunt Mary's kluski," I said without thinking.

He howled laughing and choked up. "They do, don't they!" and we both laughed.

"OK, now get some of those noodles in your can and let's get home."

I did.

Trick or Treat

We were lucky; it was a warm night, no rain and no school in the morning. The moon was full and the ghosts and goblins were running back and forth across the streets carrying pillowcases stuffed with candy, popcorn balls, apples, and oranges. Most kids were going around the neighborhood in small groups; it was more fun if you had other kids with you. We were doing the same thing.

Kasz, Gene, and I were walking slowly up one side of the street and down the other making sure we went to every door. Gene was a pirate with an eye patch and a fake moustache. Kasz wore an old black bowler hat, bib overalls, and a mop dyed red covering his hair; a set of Dave Garraway nose and glasses completed his disguise. I had my sister's old prom dress, blond wig, and makeup. I wore Keds, not high heels so I could keep up with the guys.

"Still two more blocks till we're done," Gene groaned.

His pillowcase was so filled it was ready to explode.

"Come on you guys, hurry up. The little kids are getting all the good stuff," said Kasz as he picked up speed.

I had to run to keep up with him. "Yeah, OK, we're coming," I yelled as he dashed up another set of stairs to the porch.

He barely hit the top when the front door burst open. Mr. Sendarek stormed out and yelled, "You kids leave one more bag of shit on my porch and I'll call the cops on yeh."

"We didn't do anything," Kasz said. "We're getting here for the first time." All of us came to a sudden stop next to Kasz and shook our heads along with him.

"Really, we just came down Rockwell. We just started on this block, honest," I said.

"Well, whoever's doing it is going to get his ass beat if I catch 'em." He turned and started to close the door.

"Trick or treat?" blurted Gene.

We all froze.

Mr. Sendarek stopped, smiled slightly, and reached inside for the bowl of candy and said, "Go ahead, take a bunch, you guys look pretty good. So do you, little lady."

"I'm a guy," I said.

Gene and Kasz laughed. My face turned red.

Mr. Sendarek looked again, smirked, and said, "Well, whoever you guys are, I've been yelling at kids all night instead of giving this stuff away, so take a bunch. But I'll tell ya right now that if I catch that little son of a bitch that's been ringing my bell and leaving a burning bag of shit on the porch, I'll probably kill the little bastard. It took half an hour to get my shoes cleaned up the first time it happened."

Kasz and I looked at Gene who was standing in front of Mr. Sendarek as he closed the door. Gene nodded his head, turned, and walked back down the stairs.

We followed, still packing the extra Baby Ruths he gave us into the bulging pillowcases.

"What was that all about?" I asked. The other guys shrugged their shoulders.

"Sounds like somethin' Davie might do," said Gene.

"Yeah, but, it would be funny to watch someone stomp on a flaming bag of dog shit," I said.

Everyone nodded.

There was one other place, down near California, where we saw a burned paper bag with dog shit on a porch. "Looks like he was down here too," Kasz said.

"I wonder how many bags he put out around the neighborhood," Gene said.

"Must have been lots. I wonder where he gets all the shit. I've never seen a shit store," I answered.

"Why don't you think about that tonight and tell us tomorrow," Kasz laughed. I didn't say anything.

We still had another hour of climbing stairs and collecting our share of the Halloween loot around the neighborhood. We ran from house to house, but it was getting late and the little kids were going home and not trying to beat us every place.

At the far end of Cortez, we started back toward my house. By the time we got to the Silverstein's building, we had slowed down and were also ready to stop for the night.

Only a few small clusters of costumed kids were still on the street. We could hear them being called home by their parents. The nice weather made it hard to get them home early, so parents were more relaxed about a finishing time.

Many porches and stoops had small knots of parents talking and drinking beer while they waited for the last stragglers with stuffed pillowcases to get home. They knew that once they got there, the real work of the evening would begin. Sorting candy, fruit, and money into piles was a big job. Getting anybody to wait until morning to do it was not going to happen. They wanted to sample everything. Sorting piles of candy, they didn't eat while walking around doing their collections was impossible. There was lots of crying and yelling before the whimpers quieted down for the night.

Our neighborhood was long on treats and short on tricks. Not many bad things happened, except for the occasional soaped car window or overturned trashcan—at least since Davie had been away at reform school for lighting the cat's tail on fire last year.

All of our pillowcases were overflowing with candy when we split up for the night a few minutes later. We all headed home to sort out the piles of treats. Trick or treat in my new neighborhood was pretty good, much better than by my buscias on Throop Street: lots of candy and even some pennies, nickels, and a few dimes.

"See you guys tomorrow at church," I told them as we waved goodnight. "I'll have an answer for you then."

"Church?" they said.

"Yeah, remember, tomorrow's a holy day, no school but Mass."

"Gee, I almost forgot. Thanks a lot for reminding me," Gene said.

"Yeah, thanks a lot," added Kasz.

"Hey, if I have to get up to pray for all the souls, you guys aren't going to be sleeping."

By quarter of eight the next morning, I walked down Cortez Street to St. Mark's Church. I counted three other porches that had pieces of paper bags, dog shit, and soiled shoes out front. One other concrete stoop on the same block was already washed off. This guy was really doing some serious damage. It was not funny anymore. Lots of people had to work hard to get their front doors cleaned up for no good reason.

I got to the church and looked around: neither Kasz nor Gene was there. Thirty minutes later, all the dead people were prayed for, Mass was over, and I started for home and breakfast. I had a whole day with nothing to do, except some homework and make sure dinner was ready on time. It was my night to make calf's liver, so my mother would be really mad if everything wasn't ready when she got home.

About nine o'clock Gene called. "Well, what's the answer?"

"I don't have an answer yet, but I'll bet we could find out today if we do some detective work. You interested?"

"Yeah, sounds good."

"OK, call Kasz and see if he wants to come over and join us. I would have asked you earlier, if you guys had been at Mass."

"Very funny. I'll call him and see you in about an hour."

"Good, I'll be here; that is, if you guys don't go to Hell before then for missing Mass."

The line went dead.

An hour later we were all sitting on my front stoop.

"OK, how we gonna start?" Gene asked.

"How bout we just knock on Davie's door and ask him?" Kasz suggested.

"Yeah, sure. Just say, 'Hey, Davie, glad to see you're back from boy's school. You putting bags of dog shit on porches last night?' That'd be a good opener," I offered.

"Come on guys, I'm just saying, it looks like something Davie would do so let's figger out a way to have him tell us he did it," said Gene.

"Why do we even care?" Kasz asked.

"Well to start, we got blamed for doing it last night; second, lots of people got bags on their porches; and last, it sounds funny but dog shit is really hard to clean up. It's really not very nice to do," I said.

"Why do we care who did it, really?" said Gene.

"I'm just curious now, and I don't like getting blamed for something I didn't do," I said.

"Let's walk around and see just how many places bags were left. You guys think we'll find more than the six I already know about?"

"I don't know, let's go find out," said Kasz.

We split up. I took Cortez, Washtenaw, and north on California. Kasz took Rockwell and Thomas, and Gene did the north side of Augusta and part of California. It took us about an hour to walk around, see if any messes were still there, and ask people if they had any shit on the porch last night.

"OK, so we have a total of eighteen bags of shit that we know about from only last night," Gene said, looking up from the sheet of paper he used to write the totals from each of us.

"Yeah, a few people on Washtenaw said that it happened a few other times in their buildings but not last night," I said.

"I had a few like that also," offered Kasz.

"Wow, it's like some kind of epidemic," Gene said.

"More like a shit storm," Kasz laughed.

"It looks like most of the bags are closer to our block than farther away," said Gene, looking at the paper with the numbers and addresses we collected.

"If it's on our block, you can bet Davie's involved," I said.

OK, let's go see if he's around. Maybe we can get him to tell us if he's been doing it," said Gene.

"Yeah, good idea. It's almost noon already; he should be up by now," I commented.

We walked down the block toward Davie's house. Sure enough, he was outside sitting on the primer-painted frame of a motorcycle that didn't have a motor, fenders, or gas tank. He was tightening the handlebars when we walked up. He had on blue jeans, black boots, and a ratty-looking gray T-shirt with grease streaks on the front. It looked like he just got up and hadn't even combed his hair.

"Hey, Davie, how's it going?" I asked.

He looked over at us and nodded but said nothing. He kept turning the wrench on the big bolt that held the frame to the front wheel.

"Whatcha doin'?" I continued.

"What's it look like, Dickie?"

"Working on a motorcycle, I guess."

"Boy, aren't you the genius."

"Hey, no offense, we're just going down to play some ball, thought you might want to come."

"Naw, I got to finish this thing by tonight."

"OK, we got a late start today after being out last night doing trick or treat. Did you go out?"

He laughed. "Oh yeah, I was out."

"Did you get much stuff? We sure did."

He smiled. "I think I gave out more than I got."

"Oh, so you were waiting for the kids at home and gave out candy?"

"I was out giving treats to my special friends more than getting them. Kind of like Robin Hood."

"Did you wear a costume?" Gene asked.

"Yeah, I was the Phantom. I gave out more shit than anybody in the city."

"Wow," said Kasz. "What were you passing out?"

"If you weren't on my delivery list, I can't tell you. If you were, you won't ever forget that I was there."

"Sounds like it was a special night for you," I offered.

"You bet it was. Can't wait to do it again."

"Well, if you need any help next time, let me know," offered Gene. "I like to do special things for people."

Davie laughed a bit too loud. "Sure, if you really want to help next time, I'll give you a call." He turned back to his motorcycle and didn't pay any more attention to us standing there.

We continued walking down the block to the schoolyard.

"He as much as told us he did it," Gene said.

"Yeah, but he didn't say it, did he?" I answered.

"Listen, we all know he was dying to tell us he did it but he wants to keep it all a mystery. You were right, there's no question in my mind that Davie did it, but so what? We think we know who did it but who are we going to tell?" said Kasz.

"We're going to tell nobody. One day he'll get caught," I said. "Remember the last time the cops came to pick him up? He said that those people that snitched on him would get what was coming to 'em. Well, maybe some of them were on his delivery list last night. They can tell the cops and let them figure it out. If we did, they can."

Everyone thought about that for a few moments.

"What we do know now for sure is that it's better to stay away from him. That's one guy that spreads around more shit than anyone we know."

The Beach

"Only rich people go to Oak Street Beach," my sister told me. "You go to North Avenue Beach; it has lots more sand and people from the neighborhood."

"OK, we just want to have fun," I answered.

"Take the Division Street bus all the way to State then get off and walk straight down to Oak Street Beach. You need to go under the Outer Drive. Just turn to the left when you get to the other side and walk up the breakwater, you'll see the boathouse. That's where you'll want to be."

"Sounds easy."

"It is. Don't try coming home up North Avenue. I don't want you getting lost your first time there."

"We'll be fine."

"OK. Here's the money Mom left for you," she said, handing over three quarters. "She said not to spend all of it if you don't have to."

I added up what it would cost me for the day. Twenty cents for the bus ride there and back, a quarter for a hot dog, and a dime for a drink was all I needed. So I should have another twenty cents to spare.

Gene and I were going to the beach for the very first time alone. We had both graduated from eighth grade at St. Boniface on June twenty-first . We were going to start the summer right, with a trip to the beach. I was supposed to meet him at the bus stop on Rockwell at eight thirty.

I had a brand new beach towel that my mom got at Walgreens, my swim trunks, some mineral oil with iodine to prevent sunburn, and my Cubs cap. Maybe I would stop at Ackerman's to get an apple or something else to take with us, only if the younger brother was there. I rolled up my stuff into the flamingo-covered bright green towel and ran the three blocks to the bus stop.

Gene was already there. I could see that the bus was only half a block away. There was no time for an apple. As we passed the store, I only saw the older brother inside, so there wouldn't have been an apple anyway. He was not nice like his younger brother.

The bus was really crowded. People were still going to work. We had to stand until Ashland Avenue, where everyone got off for the subway to the loop. One lady kept poking me with her shopping bag and glared at me when I pushed it away. She didn't seem very happy standing there in high heels and dress clothes and sweating before she even got off the bus.

"Window," Gene called as we followed the rush of bodies toward the exit at the back of the bus.

"Way home," I yelled. We pushed into the seat across the aisle from the exit door.

We passed right by my old neighborhood off Noble Street, under the train tracks and past the factories and the bridge over the Chicago River. I could see Goose Island on the right side of the bus already shimmering in the heat. Clouds of steam, soot, and mist rose from the weed-covered fields and buildings scattered along the banks of the river. The big, round gas and oil storage tanks west of the river stood above everything on the island.

We were quickly past my old neighborhood and into block after block of rather dirty-looking factories, warehouses, repair shops, stores, and buildings. We crossed streets I had heard about like Clybourn and Elston Avenue. Before we knew it, the buildings became brighter, newer looking, and taller as we started getting close to State Street. That's where another subway line crossed under Division Street going from Evanston to downtown. We got off with the people transferring for the loop.

"Look at those apartment buildings," I said to Gene, as I looked down the street toward the lake.

"Some of them are houses, not apartments."

"They can't be. They're too big."

"They are though; it's the rich part of town. Look, they only have one mailbox in front of this one," he said, pointing up at the three-story, gray, stone building with black trim, black wrought iron fencing, and flower boxes on the windows.

"There's dozens of them like that around here," I said.

"Probably hundreds is more like it."

"I'll bet they're really something inside."

"Yeah, well you'll never get to see them."

"Who knows? It might happen."

"No it won't, unless you have lots and lots of money."

"These people live here, so there's a chance that you could too, if you work hard."

"Are you kidding? These people are the bosses. We had them in the Ukraine too; they're different than us. You never get where they are."

"Come on, Gene. This is America. You can do whatever you want. All you have to do is work hard."

"My dad says they control stuff here the same way they did back home. There's no way you can be like 'em."

"You really believe that?"

"Sister Theon told us at graduation that there is 'dignity in labor.' Right?"

"Yeah, so what?"

"My dad said that she was preparing all of us to just be workers our whole lives, not wishing us well in our future."

"Really! I thought she was just wishing us well whatever we did. I didn't see it like that."

"He studies these things at the union hall. They know how these bosses make it hard for us to get ahead."

"I hope that's not true. This is America; we can do anything if we want to."

"We just got to the Outer Drive," I said and pointed to the right. "Hey, there's the beach. Let's get down the stairs and up the other side. I'll race you."

We ran down and under the six lanes of traffic and up onto the concrete breakwater that extended north as far as we could see. To our right was a small area of sand that was Oak Street Beach.

It was supposed to be the place where only rich people went. It didn't look any different to me. Neither did the people laying around on towels and blankets. There were a few beach chairs here and there and even an umbrella or two scattered around. It was noisy from the cars and buses on the Outer Drive next to it. I sure didn't want to stay there very long.

"Let's get going before all the good spots are taken," I said as we walked north along the water's edge. You could see the rocks on the bottom of the lake the whole way going to the boathouse where North Avenue Beach started. The water looked really deep.

The lake was really clean looking. I hoped so because we got all our drinking water from it. You could see the water cribs out in the lake what looked like a few miles off shore from the beach. I looked out at it and thought: *Could I swim all the way out there and back? Maybe after another year at Camp Channing and swimming across Scott lake, I could do it. No question.*

"Let's go down past the boathouse by the overpass," said Gene.

"Yeah, it doesn't look too crowded there."

The wooden boathouse looked like an old steam ship that someone had dragged up on shore. There were smokestacks, iron railings on the second floor, and portholes instead of windows. A small sign on it said it had been built just before I was born, but it still looked pretty good. You could change clothes, shower, and get food there.

The sand in front of the boathouse was about half-full of kids and parents. We looked for a woman that looked like a mother who would watch our things while we went in the water. "Can you watch our stuff?" I asked the woman with two small kids who were digging in the sand.

"Uh, sure. Don't be gone too long. We're leaving in about half an hour."

"OK, we're going to change and be right back. Thanks." We ran off to the boathouse changing rooms.

Ten minutes later we were back. She was gone. So were our towels, my hat, and suntan lotion. Nobody around had seen her leave either. We scouted around looking for her but she was really gone.

"See what I told you about trusting people," Gene said angrily.

"She looked OK. She even had kids with her."

"So what. She's gone. Took our stuff. You didn't leave your money did you?"

"Nah, that's in my swim suit pocket. My mom is going to kill me. She just bought that towel yesterday."

"Well, let's at least see what the water's like," Gene said. "We can always just let the sun dry us off."

149

We moved to the water holding our shoes and clothing. We walked slowly between the stretched-out bodies covering almost every inch of sand to the water's edge.

"God, that's cold!" I screeched. I ran a few feet into the water, stopped, and looked around. I was the only one in the water. Thousands of people were on the sand but only me in the water. I raced back out shivering.

"Your turn," I said to Gene.

"Sissy," he yelled, running full speed into the small waves and diving into the knee-deep water.

"I'm freezing!" was all he could say between chattering teeth as he ran out. In less than a minute, it had his lips blue and his toes numb.

"Who said the beach was fun?" he asked.

"I dunno."

"Well whoever it was didn't go in the water. No wonder everyone is crowded on the beach; it's too cold to get wet."

"It's not even noon yet and I'm kind of ready to go home," I said.

"Why don't we just walk around for a while, look over the park before we go?"

"OK, let's use the overpass over there," I pointed across the beach.

We walked by people that were white with red outlines on their arms and necks from their shirts, really red stomachs and backs from laying in the sand and a few all covered up with beach towels reading books, eating sandwiches, and drinking pop.

I got hungry.

"We should eat before we go over the bridge," I told Gene.

Soon we were standing in line at the boathouse food window. I ordered a hot dog and a root beer. Gene did the same. When it came I was shocked to find only a hot dog with nothing but a cold bun.

"Excuse me," I told the guy at the window. "You forgot to put everything on it."

"Listen kid," he answered. "We've been serving them like this for fourteen years, take it or leave it. You can get brown mustard over at the other counter. That's it. No refunds." He walked away.

Gene and I looked at each other. This was not how the day was supposed to go.

We got some mustard and took our stuff to look for a place to eat. The dogs were cold and spicy and the root beer was warm and way too sweet. I thought about the hot dog stand in my old neighborhood; *now those were hot dogs.*

We ended up sitting on the steps going down to the sand with our feet in a puddle of water from a fountain that was leaking. At least we got some of the sand off before we started putting our sneakers on.

We walked around the park for a while but decided that we would probably have more fun at home.

We retraced our way back along the breakwater toward Oak Street Beach. Even the concrete breakwater was now filled up with people sitting around reading, talking, and hanging on to the lake access ladders that were scattered along the water's edge. We didn't see anybody that went below their knees into the swells. I think they would turn blue in a minute if they did.

Gene didn't talk much as we walked back to the bus stop on State Street. He didn't say much until we were stopped back at Noble Street waiting for the traffic light to turn green.

"Look over there," he shouted.

I turned to look where he was pointing, just as a big man wearing a bar apron was throwing a guy down the steps of the corner bar. There were a few customers standing behind the bartender yelling at the guy who bounced down the cement stairs and fell into the street.

The bus started up and the scene was quickly behind us.

"Wow, I'll bet that bartender was in the Marines. He was really strong. I wonder what that guy did to get thrown out of the tavern," Gene said.

I shrugged but wondered if the guy on the sidewalk was hurt.

Gene lived close to Western Avenue so he got off first.

"See ya later," I told him. "Want to meet up after supper?"

"I'll call you when my mom gets home from work."

"OK." And he was gone.

It was only 2:30 when I got home. Nobody else was there, so I cleaned up, ate some celery with French dressing, raisins, and a few glasses of milk.

I put the twenty cents left over on the kitchen counter and went to see if anyone was down at the schoolyard. I knew how things worked there.

Humboldt Park

It's the largest park west of Goose Island. It was a place that held memories, stories, and attachments for me. I was only there once while living at my busica's house, marching in a big parade. It later became a place where I played, learned that I didn't like fishing but that tennis was OK, and almost broke several bones riding on the hilly bike trails. I also learned that making money was not as easy as it looked.

"We're wearing red-and-white neckerchiefs next week for the parade," our cub-master said. "I'll have them for you when we get ready to start marching from Nobel Street at ten o'clock. Be here by nine thirty ready to march. We're going up Division Street from Ashland to Humboldt Park in the Kościuszko Day Parade. Leave your yellow-and-blue scarves at home."

I had just joined the pack at Holy Trinity Church. It was my first week. I was still learning the Cub Scout oath, how to salute, stand in a line, and learn about stuff in the forest. It was my first parade.

I told my mom and dad our pack was marching. Mom was happy but Dad was not. He didn't like things that looked like the army but since it was for Kościuszko, he was not too mad about me walking a long way wearing a uniform.

"Did you know that Tadeusz Kościuszko was a hero in the American Revolutionary War?" my dad said.

"Really, he fought with George Washington?"

"Tak, there are lots of famous Polish people who helped America."

"Who else?"

"Well, another Pole, Casimir Pulaski, saved George Washington's life during that same war."

"Really."

"Yes, they even named a street for him right here in Chicago, Pulaski Road, on the west side."

"Wow, any others?"

"Uh hum, Paderewski was a famous composer and diplomat, and lots and lots of others. Kościuszko even helped build West Point, the military school for the Army. So, you should be proud to march. You know why they have the parade?"

"Uh uh."

"Once a year everyone marches to Humboldt Park so they can take him off his horse."

"Why do they do that?"

"So he can go number two," he said and laughed.

"Is that true?"

"No, but that's the joke we tell as the reason for having everyone march three miles in the sun wearing uniforms."

"Oh."

"Anyway, be proud you're Polish and you're marching."

"Yes, sir."

"Tak."

———

The Cub Master gave us our scarves; everybody got in line and off we went. It was hot but most of our pack finished the hike, listened to some speeches that we really couldn't hear very well, and had a picnic on the grass near the lagoon. A bus picked up the kids that didn't finish the whole march. It brought them to the park for the picnics and speeches.

Only two fat kids and one with palsy couldn't walk all the way. One of the fat kids fell down around Damen Avenue but the other one made it all the way to Western before he had to stop and wait for the bus. The kid with palsy kept walking back and forth across the street. I'll bet he walked twice as long as everyone else because he couldn't walk in a straight line. He pooped out just before California even though everyone along the sidewalk was cheering for him to finish.

The kids in the pack were kind of joking before we started marching that maybe we should get Wally's kid brother, who had polio, to come

153

with us. He was in an iron lung most of the time. They said we might be able to decorate it with some Polish and American flags and push it up Division Street to the park. Everyone thought it was a great idea until they remembered that you needed electricity to make it work. We forgot that idea, and he stayed at home. Nobody ever told him, so he was not sad that he couldn't come with us.

Except for the parade, we didn't go to Humboldt Park when we lived on Troop Street because it was too far away. When we moved away from my grandmother's house to west Cortez Street, it was only about eight blocks from our front door. It was an easy bike ride.

The park is really big. Once you cross Division Street and California, you can stay in the park for miles and miles. Fishing and trail racing were fun things you could do without anyone else or with a bunch of friends. I did lots of both.

Wally and I went fishing every once in a while but neither of us wanted to spend too much time doing it. The fish were small and it was kind of boring sitting on the bank of a lagoon watching a red-and-white bobber till something bit your worm or dough ball. We caught some crappies and a few catfish but by the time we got them home, they were already starting to spoil. I went a few times alone, early in the morning to see if my luck was any better; it wasn't. I really tried to like fishing; it just didn't like me back.

Biking was a different story.

———

"Sure it will sound like a motor bike?"

"Yeah," Wally answered while clipping the clothespin on the rear frame of my bike. He stuck an ace of diamonds into the end and pushed it part way into the wheel spokes.

I pushed the bike forward and the *thwap, thwap* sound was loud and clear.

"Let's go!" I yelled, jumping on the bike and heading toward the park. The unmistakable sound of a motorbike was right there with me. Wally followed, his bike roaring away right behind me.

We made a few noisy loops around the park, up to North Avenue, across and around the lagoons then back to California. My card broke in half just as we were rounding the last corner and my bike went silent. Wally kept on purring along.

"Look at those kids," he said, pointing toward the bush-covered hills that faced Division Street. Half a dozen bikes came racing out between a break in the bushes, flew across a sidewalk, sped up another hill, and then disappeared into the bushes. We followed them.

"Careful Wally, these branches are close to the trail," I said ducking under a low-hanging tree branch.

"OK, I'll try not to hit any of them," he said, swerving and twisting to miss it. He hit it anyway. It banged him right in the chest and knocked him off his bike. The bike crashed into the tree and the handlebars bent at a funny angle.

I braked hard and jumped off to see what happened to him. "You all right?"

He was on the ground looking up at the tree.

"Wally, Wally, you OK?"

"Wow. That was just like in Robin Hood, knocking the sheriff's men off their horses in Sherwood Forest."

"You OK?"

"Oh, yeah, I'm fine."

"I don't think your bike is so good."

"Let's look at it."

"The handlebars are bent."

"It's fine, I'll show you."

Actually he was right. He stood it up, straddled the front tire facing the frame, and twisted the handlebars straight again.

"See, no problem."

We saddled up and continued riding, a lot more slowly through the rest of the trails around the park. It probably took us an hour or so to make the first trip using the paths in the bushes. There were some really tricky places, but most of it was pretty easy if you knew which way the path twisted and turned.

"Let's practice a few more times then let's race. There are lots of places to pass each other along the trail; it should be fun."

We used the clock in the window of the cigar and magazine store on the corner of California and Division to time our races. By the end of the summer, I could make it all the way around in twenty minutes but Wally always beat me.

It was really fun whizzing through the bushes, flying down the hills, and scaring old men going number one in the bushes. Some of them peed on their pants trying to turn away from us flying by.

We tried it a couple of times when it was getting dark. Once I hit a bush and got knocked off in the first few minutes. We decided it was just too dangerous, even with our bike lights on.

———

I was starting high school in the fall. My parents thought I needed to earn some spending money, so I started looking for things to do. One of Wally's high school friends, Greg, had a Tribune paper route but wanted to give it up. He told me I could make twenty-five dollars a week on his route but I had to make the collections myself. The tips were supposed to be good because all the people were old.

About half of the papers needed to be taken to the third floor: some in the front, others in the back. Some had to be inside the front hallway, others just on the front porch. It was all on the route cards that he gave me. Collections had to be made every Friday for that week.

"I didn't get a paper on Sunday." "None on Thursday and Saturday." "It wasn't where it was supposed to be." Typical complaints regardless of whether or not I knew the paper was in the right place or not. Someone always wanted to get a paper for free. The bad thing was that it came out of my earnings.

The route boy paid for what was on this route whether the customer got it or not. Instead of making twenty-five dollars a week, I was lucky to make ten to fifteen dollars, including tips. The tips were not that great, exactly because the people were old and couldn't afford big tips. I kept the route for almost two months and then just quit. Nobody wanted to take it over, and I was going to start high school. No more time after school during the week. I don't know what the Tribune did to get the papers to all those people, but I'll bet they were complaining about whatever they were charged.

Even on the route, I could see the park on my right side all the way to North Avenue then down a block and back south toward Division Street. There were lots of trees and really nice apartment buildings along the way. Too bad lots of the people there were not very nice.

The park had lots of places to play, ball fields, tennis courts, lagoons, and big, grass-covered places. Except when it was covered with snow, the park was always busy. In the summertime people would bring picnics to the park, and the Park District had day camps so the neighborhood kids would just hang around and play. There were lots of water fountains all over the place but not many places to get a hot dog, pop, or ice cream inside the park. The guys with ice cream pushcarts were always around to make sure nobody went without something cold.

Most of the guys that pushed the carts around were DPs from somewhere trying to sell whatever they could to make some money. It looked like a great job: in the sunshine all day and making lots of money because the ice cream was pretty expensive. The company that owned the carts was over on North Avenue. They had a sign up looking for guys to sell their ice cream. Wally and I decided to try it.

"So we need to rent the cart for the day for five dollars, then buy all the stuff we're going to sell from them for another twenty-five dollars, then we got to sell all of it to make money. Is that right?" Wally asked.

"Yeah, that's it. Except we have to do it in one day, then return the cart or it will cost another five dollars."

"How much can we make a day doing this?"

"If we sell everything, we make fifty-five dollars."

"Yeah, but what about paying for the cart and ice cream? That's thirty dollars."

"OK, there are two of us, so each of us will still make twelve fifty a day."

"If we don't sell everything, what happens?"

"You can eat it or throw it away is what the guy told me. But usually everything is gone."

"Can you get fifteen dollars from your mom to try it tomorrow? I'll ask my mom."

We both got the money after some pleading and we were over on North Avenue to pick up our cart by eight o'clock the next day. It was really hot and the ice cream sold like crazy right from the start. Around noon it started to cloud up, and by one o'clock it started to pour. It rained the rest of the day. We sold nothing else.

"How many left?" I asked Wally again, not believing his count. We were sitting under an awning at the boathouse, watching sheets of water pouring down.

"Looks like exactly half of what we got this morning."

"So if we take the cart back now, we make nothing. If we wait to see if it stops, it might cost another five dollars and still sell nothing."

"Right."

We decided to take the cart back to the warehouse through the rain.

Dumping those leftover ice creams in the garbage at the factory was really hard. We tried taking some of the extras home, but they melted before we got two blocks.

We wasted a day but at least could pay our moms back. It looked like those guys with the carts charged high prices because they never knew what would happen with the weather.

I was sure glad that school was starting soon; I couldn't afford being on vacation.

The Drug Store

"Sure thing, wait a few minutes and I'll get it for you," I told Mrs. Goldman.

I took her prescription bottle into the back of the store, found the large bottle of pills, counted them out, put some new cotton in the top of her bottle, and walked back to the counter.

"Here you are, good as new," I told her. "That'll be three dollars and sixty cents."

"So much?" she said.

"If you don't want the whole thing today, I can give you less. How many would you want?"

"Could I have enough till the welfare money gets here?"

"Sure, that's on Wednesday, right?"

"Smart boy," she said. I took the bottle and counted out her twelve small green Digitalis pills, put the balance into the large bottle, and returned to the cash register.

"Here you go, Mrs. Goldman. That'll be one dollar and twenty cents today."

She carefully counted out her money from a small black change purse, took her pills, and left the store.

It was a typical Sunday morning in 1956 and I was running the neighborhood pharmacy, a great job for a sixteen-year-old high school junior. My boss, the storeowner, Samuel Yufit, known to me only as 'Sam,' would not arrive before 1:00 p.m.

Since Sunday mornings generally were not busy and I had been working at the store for two years already and was already considered an apprentice pharmacist, I could legally fill prescriptions, compound drugs, and basically run the store when he was not there.

159

The pharmacy was on Chicago Avenue, about two blocks east of Ashland Avenue close to where I graduated from St. Boniface School. Many of my customers were the parents of kids I graduated with from school and knew from church, even though my family had moved farther west as the old neighborhood had started to change. It was no longer just Polish, Russian, and Ukrainian but now had lots of Latin Americans and black people living there. But many of our customers still only spoke their native languages, not English. It was not uncommon to have six or seven languages going back and forth at any one time in the store.

Samuel Yufit was a Russian Jew who immigrated to the US. He trained there as a pharmaceutical chemist and was licensed in Illinois to operate a pharmacy, which in this neighborhood meant acting as a doctor for a large portion of the people living there.

He was an old-fashioned, European-style druggist selling what immigrants were comfortable using. Leeches for a black eye or bruise, Epsom salts for a twisted ankle, or an enema set for an all-purpose internal cleaning out. Each solution was recommended in personal consultation between the patient and Sam, and sometimes with me.

The store sold botanicals, leeches, chemical compounds, salves, elixirs, patent medicines, and modern drugs, depending on what a patient needed, what was prescribed by their doctor, or what they could afford.

It was not uncommon to have a sick child brought to the cash register, have their temperature taken, throat looked at, diagnosed with a specific illness, and a special preparation compounded to treat whatever it was that the child had.

Skin rash? A coal tar and lanolin salve would work. Nighttime cough? Elixir of terpin hydrate and codeine was the sure cure. Need to lose an unwanted pregnancy? Several choices were available to cause almost instant bleeding and abortion.

We did not have a soda fountain but lots of cosmetics, hair colorings, permanents, nylon stockings, and shaving equipment. There were all manner of surgical, latex, and rubber appliances, including trusses that Sam personally fitted.

On weekends we were very busy, especially when every other customer would only speak with Sam in the back room. It took a few years before they started asking me "What can I do for....?" It was about this time that Sam started allowing me to open the store for him on Sundays. In this neighborhood trust was more important than age or where you came from. If you were trusted the way Sam was, bringing a sick child to him was a natural thing to do. It rubbed off on me

I learned very quickly to understand the mumblings of the guys who came in to get "rubbers" or the young girl buying Kotex for the first time. I learned to put things into a bag before bringing it to the counter so that other customers could not see what they were buying. It put them at ease and ensured that they would return another time.

It was a little more uncomfortable the first few times that the parents of my friends came in to get condoms on Sunday mornings when Sam was not there. They had no choice: either ask me for them or not be prepared for the coming week. They started asking me, and I bagged them, took the money, and never said a word.

I did wonder how they could go to communion on Sunday morning and then buy rubbers, but I thought there must be some special regulation or something that they taught in the New Cana classes before people were married in the Catholic Church that allowed them to do both things. I never asked them about it; I just smiled and rang up the sale.

I had been working at the pharmacy about two years when we were held-up by two armed robbers. It was a Thursday evening when we normally closed at 9:00, but about seven o'clock these two guys came in and asked for Sam. I went in the back of the store, told Sam he had a customer, and began cleaning up bottles from the compounding counter.

Almost immediately Sam came back with his hands up over his head and the two guys right behind him. They were yelling that Sam should get them the cash. Sam was telling them that "everything was in the cash register." They yelled at me. "Where is the cash, kid?" I shrugged and said, "In the register. That's all we have. I went to the bank this afternoon."

"Don't bullshit me. We were watching the store all afternoon and never saw you go anywhere," said the younger robber.

"I went out the side door and down the alley to the bank. I always go that way," I lied.

"Bullshit," the older of the two said and hit Sam across the forehead with his gun. "Where's the money?" Sam staggered and fell down, but the robber grabbed him and pulled him to his feet.

161

"Come here, kid," the younger one said and waved his gun at me. "Show me around the back of the store."

The store was basically long and narrow with about 80 percent in the front and 20 percent in the back for the compounding area, prescription filling, drug storage, etc. There was a full basement under the store for storage of things that needed to be cool and everything that was not used on a daily basis. It had a low ceiling and poor lighting. It was a dank place that looked disorganized unless you understood what was there.

The younger of the two guys walked me down the long passageway to the basement door, opened it, and roughly pushed me down the stairs followed almost immediately by Sam and the older guy.

"I'm not going to ask you again, old man," the older guy said to Sam. "Where's the fucking money?"

"I told you already, I went to the bank about four. Everything is in the register."

That seemed to get the older guy really mad. He turned to me and said, "OK smart guy, then give me your wallet."

"What, you want my wallet? I'm just a kid; I don't have any money!"

"Give me your fucking wallet right now!" he said, raising his gun.

I thought about the old Jack Bennie joke, "Your money or your life," where Benny says to the robber, "Wait a minute, I'm thinking, I'm thinking," while he waved the gun at me.

I had just been given a new wallet for my birthday. It had my new driver's license, social security card, ten dollars, a condom, and a few religious pictures in it. I would be dammed if this robber was going to just take it away from me.

Without thinking very much, I said, "You want my wallet? If you really want it, go get it," and I threw it as far down the basement into a dark corner as I could.

The older robber said, "You little son of a bitch." Then he stopped, laughed, and said to the younger guy, "Let's get the fuck out of here. There's nothing else for us."

He turned to me and said, "Kid, you got some pair of balls." He turned back to Sam and said, "You need to give this kid a raise."

They ran up the stairs, turned, and said, "Don't come out of here for half an hour if you want to continue living." They locked the door and turned off the lights. We could hear them run from the back of the store.

About ten minutes later, while I was pounding on the door, a regular customer came back and opened the door for us and we called the police.

The cops told me that it wasn't smart not to give them my wallet and that I was lucky. I probably was lucky but after all, it was a new wallet, driver's license, and my money. Would you just give that to someone without a fight?

Sam was not injured too badly in the robbery. It was just a cut on his forehead and a headache for a few days. They never did find the money that was hidden in one of the slide-out shelves that we used to store drugs. However, Sam did start taking money to the bank every day after that. He also gave me a raise.

For the next three days, we had a policeman armed with a shotgun sitting in the back of the pharmacy waiting for those guys to come back. They never did. I also never told my parents about the robbery. They would not have let me go back to work.

The drug store had been open since 1934 and probably had never been thoroughly inventoried since then. As the new employee, it was one of my jobs to make sure that the floors were clean, the prescription area cleaned up every day, and the shelves and cabinets stocked with new merchandise as it arrived. Rotating stock to make sure the old stuff was sold first did not figure into how merchandise in the compounding area was stored.

Most drugs came with expiration dates, and we were supposed to sell them before they were no good. When I started cleaning and sorting, I found several bottles full of a thousand opium pills stored in a basement cabinet. I brought them to Sam and asked how I should put them into inventory. Opium was no longer prescribed by doctors and did not really have an expiration date but was very valuable. Sam said that he would personally take care of the pills.

A few days later one of the friendly drug company salesmen came to the store. Sam told him about the bottles I found and they had a heated discussion about what to do with it as all narcotics were supposed to be accounted for with the Bureau of Narcotics and Dangerous Drugs. The bottles were not in the store inventory and Sam could not remember either when or where he purchased them. Opium was also illegal to have unless you had a special license.

Every Friday we burned scrap in the alley behind the store off of Greenview Avenue. The next Friday when I was burning boxes and cardboard, Sam came out carrying the bottles of opium pills, opened them, and poured them into the fire. He told me to stir them up and make sure that they burned. "Don't let the smoke get into your nose or clothing," he said. "It could make you sick."

No kidding, I thought. *It could also make you rich if you sold it instead of burning it.*

Sam paused before going back into the store, turned to me, and as if reading my mind, said, "These bottles were worth a year's salary, but selling it was not the right thing to do. Some things should just not be done. Selling drugs like this one is not worth any amount of money. Don't you ever forget it!"

I never did.

Customers

"Roaches," Mr. Zelinski said quietly, "and bedbugs."

"OK, what color are the roaches?" I asked. "Black or brown?"

"Does it make a difference?"

"Yes, it does. The brown ones are easier to kill than the black ones; they're the worst."

"I'm not sure. They're so fast that you just see them scurry under the cabinets or icebox, but I think they are brown. But I'm not sure."

"Well, if you think they are brown, we can get away with just using this," I said, holding up a box of 3 percent malathion powder.

"What about the bedbugs? Where are they?"

"In the bed, where do you think they are?"

"No," I laughed. "I meant, are they in just a one bed, the sofa, a pullout, or a murphy bed. Are they just in one room or in the whole house?"

"Oh, I see what you mean. I didn't think it was going to be this complicated getting rid of some bugs."

"It really does make a difference where they are and what they are in because some places are easier to treat than others."

"OK, let me think for a minute." He paused, then continued, "Roaches in the kitchen, bedbugs in the bedroom and in the pullout in the living room. Oh, and there are some silverfish in the bathroom. So I guess there is something everywhere."

"Right," I answered. "Here are your options:

"You can use the powder for the roaches and silverfish, but the bedbugs are very different. You need to use Lysol and wash the mattresses where you found them. Killing each one and their eggs is really important. If you don't get all of them, they will come back very fast. You need to take all the bedding, ticking, blankets, spreads, quilts, and pierzyna

165

to a laundromat and wash them in hot water. Don't bring them home until you finish washing and drying the mattresses, bed frames, floor, and anything else that was on or near the bed. Oh yeah, don't forget the pillows; they like to hide there."

"Oh, my God."

"The other option," I continued very quietly, "is to fumigate the entire house, after you get the bedding clean and outside."

"What does it mean, fumigate?"

"Well, we only recommend it for very bad cases of bugs since it is very complicated and messy, but it works great and lasts a long time."

"What does it do? How do you do it?"

"You basically seal up the entire apartment, light sulfur candles, and leave until they burn out. As they burn they release sulfur into the air and it settles on every surface in the apartment."

"My God, you gas them?" he said, recoiling so that the dark blue number tattoo on his arm twitched.

"No, Mr. Zelinski, you don't gas them. You coat everything with poison and that kills them."

"But we can't stay in the apartment while the candles are burning?"

"That's right. Since you have three rooms plus the bath, you would need about fourteen large candles. They will burn for about three hours, so you'll need to light them and leave. They will burn out when the air is so full of the sulfur smoke that they can no longer stay lighted."

"What else do I need to finish using the candles?"

"All the metal surfaces in the house need to be coated with Vaseline. If you don't cover them well, the sulfur will turn the metal black. It will not come off!" I warned him. "You don't want that to happen!"

"After the candles are finished burning, you need to clean up all the sulfur powder so you can move back in and live there."

"How long will that take?" he almost whimpered

"It depends, but we had a customer that said she was able to clean up afterward in about a day. Her apartment was about the same size as yours," I told him.

"People actually do this?"

"Yes sir, it's either use sulfur or do the clean and wash every few weeks. Those bugs are very persistent."

"How much does it cost to use the sulfur?"

"If you already have Vaseline, the candles will cost sixty cents each or about ten dollars and forty cents. I don't know what the laundromat charges in this neighborhood but in mine, it would cost about twenty-five cents per load to wash and a dime to dry. I guess everything should cost about fifteen dollars to get the place cleaned and bug-free."

"Let me go talk to my wife and I'll stop back. How late are you open tonight?"

"Since it's Saturday, we close at seven o'clock."

"OK, see you later," he said and quickly left the store.

"Sure thing, we'll be here."

About an hour later he came back, bought the candles, Vaseline, and some Lysol. I wished him good luck and good hunting. He just looked at me trying to decide if I was being funny or not. I was, but I tried not to show it.

I had been in many of the neighborhood buildings delivering pre-scriptions to our homebound and addicted customers. The living conditions were not good in most of them. In this part of Chicago, the buildings were fifty to sixty years old, in poor condition, and not well maintained. The hallways were often dark with maybe a single light bulb hanging seven feet from the floor to illuminate long, narrow, unpainted wooden-plank floors. Each floor might have six to eight small apartments with a hard-to-read letter on the door marking the address. Sometimes the customer would just say the street number and then say, "Look for the mezuzah on the third-floor door, that's me."

Mr. Zelinski lived in one of these buildings. I didn't tell him when he was in the store about one of the major side effects of using sulfur candles; your neighbors get angry. While they may have the same problems as you with bugs, they are not happy with your using the sulfur because you will be moving your bugs into their apartments. The same bugs have probably been moving from apartment to apartment as fumigation takes place. They go where there is more to eat and fewer problems from powders, sprays, and sulfur. Sulfur is by far their worst enemy and they will stay away from it for up to a year, unless your neighbor uses it again, forcing them to move back in with their old friends.

He would learn about this problem but still be thankful for the bug-free six to twelve months he got for his fifteen dollars.

167

Many of our customers came from this neighborhood. Most of the buildings were three or four stories and had stores or shops on the first floor if they were on main streets. If they were on side streets, they had a Chicago basement plus four floors of walk-up apartments. As many as twenty-five or thirty families lived in a single building sharing their cooking odors, radio programs through the walls, and bugs, rats, and any other shared inconveniences of the season: frozen windows in the winter, sweltering heat in the summer, poor water supply, never any hot water, and diseases that spread like fire on oil. You could smell the residue of current and past attempts to eradicate different types of bugs and pests. There was a cloying sweet smell of sulfur, DDT, and the host of other chemicals used to try keeping an apartment pest free. Unfortunately the only thing that really worked was moving to another neighborhood, everything else was just a temporary solution.

There were lots of temporary solutions sold in the drug store. There were packages to keep your hair from getting gray, getting straight, or away from places that it was not wanted. More importantly there were lots and lots of preparations to keep reality from closing in.

———

"Take this prescription to Mrs. Jankowsky," Sam said, handing me the pint-sized bottle of phenobarbital elixir.

"OK, I'll get it right over to her," I told him, taking off my white jacket and putting on my winter coat.

"She is probably not going to like what you are bringing her," he said.

"Why is that? It looks like a full bottle," I said, holding the bottle up to the light.

"She is expecting two bottles, so she might be angry," he warned.

"She's OK when she comes in here to refill the prescription."

"That's right, but I talked with her and she is off on a bender and wants to have a double refill so she doesn't have to come to the store so often."

"Ah," I said. This was my first delivery to her apartment, as well as the first time she was not acting normal.

"Every once in a while she takes more than she is supposed to, so I try to cut back her medication without getting her too angry. Once before she went crazy and drank the whole bottle and the firemen with the pull motor had to pump her stomach and take her to County. They kept her there for a month to dry out."

"Oh, I didn't know."

"Well, not many people know but since you're going over there, you need to know her history."

"Anything else I should know?" I asked, as I was moving toward the front of the empty store.

"Just be careful going over there. Her neighbors know she uses phenobarbital and some of them like to steal it from her. Make sure they don't take it away from you before you give it to her."

"OK!" I answered but thought, *It's snowing, already dark, she lives in the last apartment on the fourth floor, three blocks from the store, and I have drugs that her neighbors like to steal. Nothing to worry about here.*

It was easy enough to find the right building. The hallways and stairs were even fairly well lit. Finding her apartment was another story, as she did not give Sam her apartment number just the floor, so I had to knock on three doors to finally get to her. Each door opening was onto a slightly different reality than the previous one. The only common thing was that they all knew Mrs. Jankowsky, just not exactly which apartment she lived in on the floor.

"Mrs. Jankowsky, Yufit Pharmacy," I shouted, knocking on the door.

The door seemed to fly open instantly and an impossibly thin, gray-looking woman appeared in the doorway. "Quiet down," she hissed. "You want everyone to know what you're bringing me?"

"Eh, good evening, Mrs. Jankowsky," I stammered.

"Did you bring it?" she quietly asked.

"Here it is," I said, handing her the bottle.

"Where's the rest?" she angrily asked.

"That's all we had on hand tonight. We are getting another order in tomorrow afternoon, unless the snow holds things up."

"I need both bottles," she started to wail.

"Sam said to tell you that he would personally get more to you just as soon as it comes in." Then I added, "And I'll bring it to you myself."

She sort of stepped back a bit and looked me over. "Say, aren't you the boy who filled my prescription the last time I was in the store?"

"Yes mam, that was me."

"Well, you seem like an honest boy. You wouldn't lie to me, would you?"

"Oh no, mam. I'll get the refill to you just as soon as we get it in the store."

She stepped real close and pulled five dollars out of her housecoat pocket and handed it to me. "Here, sonny. Keep the change but be sure to get over here tomorrow."

"I can't take tips, Mrs. Jankowsky," I told her.

"The hell you can't," she said, turned around, and quietly closed the door.

I stood there for a moment listening to her walking away from the door and hearing several of the doors along the hallway click closed. Her neighbors had clearly been listening to our conversation. Now I was frightened. They knew she had her drugs and I had five dollars and four floors to get down before I was safe. I never ran down any stairs as fast as I did that night.

"Any problem finding her?" Sam said when I got back to the store.

"No...no problems at all."

"She give you a tip?"

"Ah, yes she did. She wouldn't take it back."

"Good. Keep it, you earned it tonight," Sam said, laughing.

Postscript

I t's a miracle that this book was written. By all rights it never should have happened. If it were not for the Central Phoenix Writer's Workshop, it never would have seen the light of day. The chapters started their life as short stories that I wrote to help work around writer's block while developing my first novel, *Above the Bottom Line*.

I found it was easier to write about things that I knew about rather than trying to create fiction in uncharted areas. I chose things from my youth that made an indelible mark on me.

These stories don't have any grand philosophy behind them. They are remembrances of growing up in a unique part of a big city at a special time in history. My worries were few, problems manageable, and everything new and exciting. There was nothing we couldn't do, if we worked at it.

Every kid in our neighborhood just knew that if they wanted to be a fireman, mailman, soldier, or anything, they could do it. None of the kids I played with thought about being doctors or dentists. Priests were always being touted as a good, clean job, but you needed lots of schooling to become one. Lots of girls wanted to be nurses. My sister became one.

Capturing the history, sights, and feel of these three different parts of the city was not my goal. I hoped that I could recreate what a kid living in those times, in those places, experienced and how they affected his life. There is no attempt to have an overall purpose for the stories. Each of them hopefully stands on its own as a snapshot of that time, and of those events.

I was not a very good student. I got by. I graduated from St. Philip High School and after several college attempts, finally graduated from Wright Junior College, Michigan State University, got my master's there, then a PhD. from the University of Wisconsin-Madison.

I left my mark on Chicago as a student intern from Michigan State University's School of Criminal Justice working for the Chicago Police Department's Planning Division. I drafted the department's General Order that required officers to wear the now ubiquitous checkered hatbands. Superintendent O.W. Wilson liked the study and adopted my recommendation to distinguish police officers from private security guards. I was not well liked by officers for quite a while afterward, but it did the job and it's still in use!

After graduating I became a spy for our government, as a Clandestine Services officer for the CIA. Later I worked as a university professor, corporate security executive and then an international business consultant.

My wife and I wrote many books about management, security, and protecting intellectual property. We lived in Hong Kong and Asia for many years. All of these accomplishments were built on the foundation the streets of Chicago in these neighborhoods gave to me. The stores where I worked, especially the Yufit Pharmacy on Chicago Avenue, the people who guided me along the way, and the characters who lived there, all influenced the person I became.

The pull of the city keeps me coming back regularly over the years to visit family and friends. It's too bad my old high school is now a parking lot. Fortunately St. Phillip has a strong alumni association. That's the city; physical things change. The people who live there, in the neighborhoods, change more slowly.

Richard S. Post
WWW.WestofGooseIsland.com

Glossary of Polish Terms

Babka	Kind of sponge cake with honey baked into it.
Babushkas	Old ladies
Busia (s)	Grandmother; grandmothers
Cicho	Be quiet
Co Robisz	What are you doing?
Dziekuje	Thank you
Dziennik Chicagoski	Chicago Daily Newspaper
Jestes Glupi	You're crazy; Nuts
Kluski	Thick noodles
Neitz	Nothing
Nie Rozumiem	I don't understand.
Niszse Klasy	Low class
Pierogi	Dumpling
Pierzyna	Quilt or Comforter
Szlachta	Upper class
Tak	Yes; Right; Correct

8625323R00111

Made in the USA
San Bernardino, CA
17 February 2014